Married to the Franchise

Living a Championship Life of Partnership

Jonathan A. Carroll, Ph.D.

BALBOA.
PRESS

A DIVISION OF HAY HOUSE

Balboa Press books may be ordered through booksellers or by contacting:

Balboa Press
A Division of Hay House
1663 Liberty Drive
Bloomington, IN 47403
www.balboapress.com
1 (877) 407-4847

Because of the dynamic nature of the Internet, any web addresses or links contained in this book may have changed since publication and may no longer be valid. The views expressed in this work are solely those of the author and do not necessarily reflect the views of the publisher, and the publisher hereby disclaims any responsibility for them.

The author of this book does not dispense medical advice or prescribe the use of any technique as a form of treatment for physical, emotional, or medical problems without the advice of a physician, either directly or indirectly. The intent of the author is only to offer information of a general nature to help you in your quest for emotional and spiritual well-being. In the event you use any of the information in this book for yourself, which is your constitutional right, the author and the publisher assume no responsibility for your actions.

Any people depicted in stock imagery provided by Thinkstock are models, and such images are being used for illustrative purposes only. Certain stock imagery © Thinkstock.

Printed in the United States of America.

ISBN: 978-1-4525-8573-4 (sc)
ISBN: 978-1-4525-8575-8 (hc)
ISBN: 978-1-4525-8574-1 (e)

Library of Congress Control Number: 2013919678

Balboa Press rev. date: 02/06/2014

For Mom and Dad,

a sincere thank-you for the training

Contents

Foreword

Jon Carroll and I were a part of this young, gifted, and black circle of friends who bonded at the University of Pennsylvania and were everything to each other as we journeyed into adulthood. We planned elaborate reunions after we all graduated, descending at least once a season on a crew member's house for the weekend, hitting the clubs, staying up late, and playing interactive games while sipping on vodka and Hawaiian punch (or plastic cups of white zinfandel).

I loved Jon. Not in a romantic way but in a way that gave me hope for my own future opportunity for romance and respectful, reciprocal relationships. He and the rest of the guys—Terrance, Mike, O'Neil, and Stan (all now blissfully married)—were the good ones. They were the ones we called to vent about bad dates and ugly breakups. They were the ones who rescued us from the creepy dude at the bar. They were the ones who remembered our birthdays (before Facebook was ever invented) and called to congratulate us on professional accomplishments. In short, they were our cheerleaders in the manliest sense of the word. They rooted for us to achieve and offered a strong arm of support when we attempted dangerous stunts and risked losing our balance.

When Jon first shared that he and Nkechi had begun dating through a chance encounter in New York, I immediately liked it. Not only were they both super tall, but they were extreme extroverts, highly intelligent, and damn funny. I knew Nkechi from cultural organizations and activities in which we'd both been involved at school, and we also shared the connection of graduating from college a year earlier than planned. She was a rock star on campus, majoring in economics, speaking French fluently, and representing her West African heritage with pride. It made sense that Jon was excited, especially when he shared that he'd been admiring her from afar since the first day of freshman year.

Despite my happiness for Jon's newfound relationship, their unofficial union did signify the potential end of an era. There was no way that the crew was still going to crash ten deep on someone's floor once people started having serious girlfriends. But then Jon pulled a move that no one anticipated. He brought Nkechi with him to a crew weekend. As he walked through the door of Patrice's apartment with his new other half and an extra sleeping bag in tow, Patrice and I stole a glance at each other and raised our eyebrows. The nonverbal exchange was not to suggest that Nkechi wasn't welcome but to signal the existence of a new element. We caught Mike and Terrance sharing a similar smirk.

We all knew and liked Nkechi very much, as she had been our classmate at Penn and had individual connections to many of us. But she wasn't in the Vortex, as we called it, so she still carried the status of outsider. There was no way to tell how she might respond to the crew's favorite sport—the game of Darts. The Vortex loved to throw zingers. Making fun of one another was a pastime that also became competition. Who could deliver the best dig? Who could drop the funniest reference to some past incident that the victim in no way wanted to remember?

We initiated Nkechi with Darts Lite, keeping the jokes to superficial observations, not going in for the kill the way that we often did with each other. It was Patrice's little brother, a guest himself at the party, who cast the first stone as Nkechi sat on Patrice's couch with her jeans, exposing at the ankle one centimeter of black knee-highs with a paisley print. "Yo, Jon!" Rennard shouted. "Why your girl got on church socks with jeans and a sweatshirt?"

An extended moment of awkward silence ensued before hysterical laughter. The loudest guffaws were coming from Nkechi herself. And that's when we knew that Nkechi Okoro was in the crew to stay.

The weekend that Jon and Nkechi got married in Philadelphia began with near disaster... for me. The happy couple was getting hitched in a time before wedding invitations became par for the course. We were in our very early twenties and couldn't believe that two of our friends were jumping the broom already. We were also determined to look amazing, as the soiree would serve as a college reunion of sorts, and you never knew what could develop.

I'd bought a new dress for the occasion. Their wedding was black-tie, which provided my girls and me with excuses to go all out. The gown was yellow with intricate beading and an exposed back. It was fabulous—so fabulous that when I stopped in Long Island to join the carpool leaving from New York, I brought the dress in the house to show it to our friend Dayle's mom. You probably see where this story is going.

Four grizzly hours of traffic later, we pulled up to Penn's campus in time to meet additional crew members for happy hour at our favorite margarita spot. When O'Neil popped the trunk to grab his duffel bag, I realized that my garment bag wasn't there. It was still sitting in the living room with Dayle's parents in Baldwin, New York. All of the guys minus Jon were on the scene to observe the theatrics—my panicked shriek, the blinking back of tears. Terrance and Mike even offered to chip in to purchase a new dress so that no one had to return to Long Island. But at the end of the day Dayle rode shotgun as I drove the rental car back over the Verrazano Bridge to retrieve the precious garment.

The following day's wedding ceremony was breathtakingly beautiful. Nkechi looked stunning as she hit the aisle in a strapless gown that flattered every curve. Their joy washed over the pews, and we eagerly stood at the ceremony's conclusion, waiting our turn in the receiving line to congratulate the pair. I was still several people away from Jon when I heard him shout, "Yeah, Skerritt. The dress was worth going back." Nkechi then pulled me in for a big hug, lamenting my ordeal and expressing her gratitude that I had made it.

Somehow in the hours before the wedding my ridiculous dress ordeal made it into the prenuptial dialogue, and while their day should have rightfully been all about one another, they still found ways to make the people they loved feel special and important. I realized in that moment that while I had been taking lessons for years from Jon about what it meant to be a good guy (and then what it meant to be a man in love once he met Nkechi), I was about to embark on an education in what it meant to build a franchise. If they could lift up their friends in esteem and celebration at every possible moment, then what they were capable of doing for each other as a family unit had absolutely no limit.

If you think that you're about to read the most romantic love story of all time, let's be clear. Warm and fuzzy are not words that one associates with the Carrolls. Jon and Nkechi argue. Loudly. They talk over each other, standing up indignantly, their towering frames flailing about as they fight tooth and nail to have the last word. They sure do shout, and they know how to holler. About board games.

Mostly Taboo. Game nights have been a long-standing tradition in our crew, and there is only one way that teams are determined—by gender. Jon and Nkechi enjoy serving as Taboo captains and consequently fierce opponents. This is probably the one instance where calling them Team Carroll could be considered a misnomer. A game night does not go by where one doesn't challenge the other about a questionable clue or whether a cheater tried to claim a point after the last grain of sand hit the bottom half of the hourglass.

While it can be uncomfortable to watch couples fight, everyone at game night is family. So we know how they roll. Not only are we comfortable with the noise, but we hype it up—taking sides, adding evidence, and using the Taboo buzzer to punctuate the end of particularly explosive sentences.

It came as no surprise to any of us who knows this lovingly loud, opinionated couple that Jon decided to write a book about their marriage. Having secured and grown his own "franchise player," Jon wants the same for those whom he loves. He wrote this book as a way to offer up his story to those whom he doesn't know as a way to cheer on the masses. Whether you're single and looking, partnered and struggling, or enjoying married bliss, there is a lesson, a reminder, or a familiar tune for you in *Married to the Franchise.*

It does feel a bit strange reading a book about a couple that you know personally. As I began the first chapter, I'd wondered what detail would resonate with my current life circumstance. What I ended up appreciating most when I was reading Jon's account of their journey to togetherness was the length of time that he had noticed Nkechi before they ever dated. For five years he watched and admired her without so much as mentioning to anyone but his roommates that he liked what he saw. Jon knew that she was a franchise player from informal observation and casual conversation. He stored that information until he was ready and the time was right.

What this suggested to me is that we never know when someone is studying us—the way we carry ourselves, the decisions we make, the ambitions we display, the compassion we evidence when we think no one is looking. The investment in ourselves must begin long before we meet our potential mates. We can't wait for the right person to show up to begin our own personal development. Poet Kahlil Gibran says on the subject of marriage, "But let there be spaces in your togetherness," suggesting that married folks still need to have their own passions, separate interests, and individual selves. If you are not yet comfortable in your own skin and if you don't love your own quiet company, then you will not develop your identity by merging your life with someone else's.

Jon and Nkechi's wedding was like something out of a storybook. We all joked at the time that we felt like extras in *Coming to America*, the movie where Eddie Murphy was wed in an extravagant ceremony in the fictional African country of Zamunda. Many of Nkechi's Nigerian relatives sponsored wedding favors for all of the guests, so we left the celebration with a swag bag bigger than what celebrities might expect to get at the Oscars. I don't usually remember people's anniversaries, but everyone knows the date that the Carrolls got hitched. "August 10, 2002" was printed on clocks, CD cases, and notepads along with photos and drawings of the couple's smiling faces.

But no one's marriage is a fairy tale. It surely wasn't when they had to leave behind their friends and family on the East Coast to pursue an industry that Nkechi knew she could penetrate in Hollywood. It wasn't a piece of cake when Jon enrolled in a doctoral program at UCLA, sacrificing a salary and time with their son in order to obtain the degree that he knew he would need for his own ambitious pursuits. It wasn't peaches and cream as Jon and Nkechi anxiously waited to know if they would be blessed with a child after they completed the extensive process to become adoptive parents. Yes, they are fortunate to have very happy endings to many of their struggles. But I would suggest that the outcomes have been heavily influenced by the strength of Team Carroll—the support they give one another through all.

Despite the sports references, *Married to the Franchise* is not a playbook. It is not a how-to manual describing the necessary moves to score and keep a franchise player. Instead, Jon will urge you through the telling of his own experience to be the best version of yourself that you can muster. The light that you shine onto the world will draw the right person to you. Then the real work begins as you strive to grow and improve at the same time that you must turn yourself over completely to putting your partner's needs ahead of your own. Sound impossible? I may have thought so if I didn't have friends such as Jon and Nkechi, who demonstrate that it can be done. They invest in the franchise by relentlessly pursuing their individual projects while willingly making sacrifices in service of the Team Carroll's advancement.

I called Jon after I finished reading his manuscript and thanked him for the honest life lessons. I shared the takeaways that I gleaned from his written words and expressed my gratitude for a book that was affirming to the independent, goal-driven life that I choose to lead, as opposed to some of the recently published works that tell women (especially women of color) that everything we have been doing is wrong. *Married to the Franchise* will not berate you for giving up "the goods." It will push female and male readers alike to reflect, but without the holier-than-thou lectures.

In response to my feedback, Jon shared that I, along with the rest of our crew, had educated him as well. He was better prepared for his partnership with Nkechi because of his years of being an excellent friend. "What you do leading up to your marriage impacts your marriage," he reminded me. You don't wake up one day and decide to be a strong listener or an enthusiastic cheerleader. It comes from years of practice with the people who have been in your life all along.

It's probably the most important lesson of all to remember. If we can commit to learning from and serving as supports for our friends and family, we will reap the benefits when we find and fall in love with our franchise player.

Thank you, and you're welcome, Team Carroll.

Rachel Skerritt

Author and educator

Introduction:
Franchise Player

I first met Nkechi Okoro at the University of Pennsylvania Freshman Convocation in the fall of 1995. I was immediately struck by her British accent and the fact that she stood nearly eye to eye with me at five feet eleven. (I still contend she's taller than six feet). I was knowledgeable enough to know that there were Black women all over the world who sported accents of all kinds, but Nkechi was the first with whom I had the chance to converse and hear utter my name. The height/ accent combo instantly made her a person of interest, someone to follow up with as I surveyed the full female scene at the official kickoff to the school year.

Fast forward a couple of weeks, and I again encountered Miss Okoro. This time I sat in the audience as she performed in a collection of one-act performances.

On this night, high-heeled shoes easily bumped her height to six feet two, which would intimidate some— but not me. She was rocking her A-game makeup and formfitting clothing, which accentuated all the curves that would make any man snap to attention. So now I was even more interested than our first meeting. Knowing little about her beyond her physical profile, I immediately placed Nkechi Okoro into the wife-piece category, a distinction not given lightly. It was reserved only for those women you would do whatever it took to be with. Later in my college years women in this category would be dubbed "franchise players." Little did I know as I watched her in that one-act performance how correct I was in my evaluation of Miss Okoro. As we near the completion of our eleventh year of marriage, I felt compelled to share what I've learned about partnering with such a remarkable woman and maintaining a happy marriage because we have truly been blessed.

The Mrs. and I often receive compliments about how easy we seem to make marriage look or how well we seem to complement each other. Given the work that we have done and the support that we have received along the way, it is worth explaining how we keep *Team Carroll* together. The notion of marriage is changing in this country, and the essential questions should not center solely around whether or not marriage is still relevant or if we are meant to have just one marriage. The discussion should also include questions about the ways to keep marriages healthy and thriving, ways that are not simply based in satisfying physical or financial needs. Diving into the newsstand magazine article about "10 Ways to Lick Her until She Screams" or "10 Characteristics of a Power Couple" will not get it done. In addition, the dialogue on marriage needs to have input from men because we do play a small yet important role in the marriage equation. I've been blessed to have peers and mentors who have been successful in keeping their marriages strong while pursuing professions and raising children. Their input will be sprinkled throughout the book to give balance to the way I see things. My goal is to offer up narratives of how men do this as a counter to the popular perception that we are too afraid to commit to marriage, reluctant to be emotional in our relationships, and too insecure to be with women who bring equal if not greater financial assets to the table.

Being married to a franchise player is about being secure enough to support my wife and think about our team goals while at the same time being open to her challenging me to be my best. This book is about the journey to being able to accept such a powerful love and then the roller-coaster ride that ensues on the way to fulfilling our destinies both individually and as a couple. This book is a way of saying, "Thank you," as we pass a small milestone in our journey together. I don't take it lightly that we have made it to ten years. I draw great motivation from my marriage and have invested a great deal in making sure that it never falls apart. As an avid sports fan, the franchise player metaphor has gone from a convenient parallel used by a bunch of college males to discuss women while they consume sports to a serious lens through which I can actually make critical comparisons between myself as the head of Team Carroll, Inc., and the way owners of professional sports teams behave when they are dealing their most prized partners, their franchise players. Before I get any further into this love story, let me first give you background and further explain the franchise player concept as it relates to relationships so that as you read this book, you have a clear notion of what I mean when I refer to my wife and the wives of my friends as franchise players. The intent is not for my wife to be viewed as a possession whose sole purpose is to entertain me and enhance my riches, but instead as someone whose unique skills and talents require that I am always working to be my best self in order to maintain our partnership.

Growing up in Philly, the vernacular that surrounded how you described your relationships with women was not expansive. If you were seeing someone on a semi regular basis, that was your "girl." My dad's generation might have said your "main squeeze" or your "lady." Other than that, there was the *side jawn*, who was not the main attraction but was also on your roster. This was pretty much the extent of my lady lexicon when I arrived on campus in 1995. As time went on, *wife-piece* or *wifey* became popular terms. *Wifey* became so popular that the R & B group Next made a song bearing that title. The franchise player term carries more respect than all of these.

When you hear the term *franchise player*, you immediately think of sports icons like Michael Jordan, Magic Johnson, Larry Bird, and more recently, LeBron James and Peyton Manning. As the visibility of women's team sports have grown, examples would be Mia Hamm, Lisa Leslie, Sheryl Swoopes, and Candace Parker. Franchise players are instantly identifiable with the organizations they represent and the sports they play. Their physical and mental talents allow them to lift those around them to championship-caliber performances. Their talents also allow them to enjoy an elevated status in their partnerships. Johnson enjoyed such a strong relationship with the late Los Angeles Lakers owner Dr. Jerry Buss that he was able to purchase an ownership stake of the team when he retired. In contrast, Chicago Bulls owner Jerry Krause refused to elevate Jordan's influence within the organization despite his status as the best player in the league, and ultimately Jordan left the Bulls in 1998 after they had won six championships. For the purposes of this book, a franchise player does not score points, goals, or runs, but similar to an athlete, they make use of their essence to make their families and those around them feel better and do better.

My wife is the franchise player of Team Carroll. Eleven years ago I offered Nkechi a lifetime contract by getting down on my knee with a diamond in hand. This put me in the CEO position, and thankfully the former Miss Okoro agreed to come aboard and extend my branch of the Carroll family tree. Nkechi and I work together as partners to extend the franchise through a number of different vehicles. Individually we each have our own professional and personal identities that allow us to bring resources back to the home base.

Since LeBron James joined the Miami Heat, he has elevated the organization with his individual talents and through relationships with companies like Nike, Sprite, and McDonald's. When these partnerships go well, championships follow, provided that both parties continue to do what is necessary to keep moving forward together. In these examples you see that sports vernacular maps nicely onto how we can characterize relationships, and the behavior displayed by sports franchise management and their elite players when things go wrong often matches the behavior common in romantic relationships. There is miscommunication. Needs and desires change, or personalities that once seemed complementary turn out not to be compatible.

In the fall of 1996 my college peers, and I intuitively shared this understanding of the characteristics of a good woman as we sat around our college dorm room, talking about the most recent crop of freshmen women to enter our fine university. At the time none of us perceived of how applicable this metaphor would be to our lives to the point where we are still talking about franchise players to this day, albeit with an increased level of maturity and understanding.

This text will be the first of two volumes and will be organized into three main parts—*The Road to The Altar, The Newlywed Years, and The Foundation Years.* The second volume will address the *Legacy Years* and offer tales of those who have fallen off the marriage carousel only to find their way back on. I will offer my experiences on the road to becoming a husband, and then after the wedding enhanced by insights from my married friends at similar points on their journey. I interviewed five of my trusted married friends to provide contrast and comparison to my narrative. Let me introduce them now so that you have a sense of who they are as I refer to them throughout the text.

Michael (Mike) Trent—Mike Trent was my roommate in college for three years, and then we shared an apartment together for almost two years after he graduated in 2000. He has been married for more than eight years now to his wife, Kelci, and they have two children. My goddaughter, Kaylin, is four, and her younger brother Michael is two. Mike is a chemical engineer by training and also holds an MBA. Kelci studied business in undergrad and has her own MBA. The thing that sticks out for me about the Trents is the way they both balance very busy professional lives yet maintain a stable family structure for their children. They also travel as much as any couple I know. There are not too many islands that they have not toured.

O'Neil Palmer—O'Neil is another Penn classmate who was my roommate for two years. We graduated at the same time in 1999, and then he moved to St. Louis to work for IBM. He got married in 2007, divorced in 2008, and remarried in 2012. His wife, Shani, is such a franchise player that he moved to London to be with her. The journey that O'Neil took to pick himself up emotionally after the first marriage did not work out is fascinating as is his current life abroad with his new bride.

Terrance Whitehead, a.k.a. Chico and Mr. Cheeks—The last of my college roommates from Penn also had a marriage that did not work but found a way to get back in the saddle and remarry. His current union is unique in that his bride had two children from a previous marriage. So not only did he start a new life with Kourtney when they exchanged vows, but he became a stepfather in a blended family that also includes Kourtney's ex-husband. That is a lot to take on at one time, but I know both Terrance and Kourtney will figure out how to make it all work.

Alimi Ballard—You may know him from his run on the show *Numb3rs* or from his roles in movies like *Fast Five*, but I know him as husband to Dahn and father to two beautiful children. I met him because both of our wives are members of the same mom group, and since then we have vibed on being Black fathers doing our best to raise children and keep our families together. The passion and energy with which Ali speaks made him a prime candidate for this book, and he did not hold anything back.

Royale Watkins—Royale Watkins is a comedian and the creator of the popular *Mixtape Comedy Show* staged monthly in New York. For the purposes of this book, he's one half of the most open married couple I know. One need only check out an episode of the web series *After I Do*, which he cohosts with his wife, April, to see what I mean. There is no topic that they won't address publicly from potential threesomes to spending money on their kids' education. I have always benefited from having successfully married men around me whom I could observe and talk to. Royale Watkins has become one of those guys for me since we have been in LA.

These gentlemen make up a support structure that enables me to reach out for advice or counsel on any number of issues. However, in the beginning, my central support structure consisted of my family. My parents put a lot into their firstborn, and my grandparents dove into their second turn at parenting with pride and enthusiasm.

Part 1

The Road to the Altar

Training Days

I said, "Mom, what are you doing? You're ruining my rep."
She said, "You're only sixteen. You don't have a rep yet."

—DJ Jazzy Jeff and the Fresh Prince

My parents, John and Emily Carroll, spoiled me rotten along with my sister, Jennifer, and brother, Jarad. They are both college graduates with advanced degrees, so their goal when it came to their children was to make sure we went even further than they had. My mother recently noted in a Facebook comment, "It was about providing the three of you with a solid foundation to build upon!" They worked damn hard to do this. Both were career teachers in the School District of Philadelphia (SDOP), which meant that they had to work a number of

3

side jobs to make sure that private school tuitions were paid, clothes were bought, and stomachs stayed full.

In addition to teaching industrial arts, my father served in the US Air Force Reserves for twenty years, which meant that one weekend out of the month he would go and stay at Maguire Air Force Base in Fort Dix, New Jersey. At different points he also worked at Staples, Wawa, a 24-7 convenience store, and Girard Bank. For my entire youth, his day would start at about 5:00 a.m. Before I was old enough to dress myself, he used to wash me up and get me ready for school. Once he left the house, he would stop at the 7-Eleven about a mile from the house to get his coffee, and then he would teach all day. He would come home and pass out for just over an hour before he would go work his second job until late in the evening. Finally he would come home and get ready to do it all over again the next day. On Sundays he served as a deacon at our church and sang in the choir.

My mother has an equally strong work ethic. She would be up just as early so that she could wash up in peace. She would then get us all out of bed while she ate her breakfast and listen to Jeremiah Wright sermons on the radio. By the time I was dressed and headed down to breakfast, she was doing my sister's hair. Eventually we would all end up at the kitchen table, eating breakfast, and then we would pile into the car so she could drop us all off at school. When her school day ended as an elementary math teacher, her car became the activity shuttle that carried us to swim and soccer practices, music lessons, birthday parties, or anything else on our social calendar. On Sundays while my dad was up in the choir loft, she was making sure we made it to the 7:45 a.m. service on time. When the school year ended, she would often teach summer school or work for the swim camp we attended, which was sponsored by the Philadelphia Department of Recreation. As she neared retirement from the SDOP, she worked for Bed Bath & Beyond and ShopRite, which were helpful in keeping my first apartment furnished and the fridge stocked.

I was also blessed to have my maternal grandmother, Clayvonne Close, a.k.a. "Nana," as an integral part of my life growing up. We were a swimming family, and as I got older, that meant that my practices started right after school. Instead of having me take the fifteen-minute trolley ride up Germantown Avenue from Germantown Friends School (GFS) to the Marcus Foster Recreation

Center, Nana would pick me up every day. She would drop me off at the pool and head back to my house, where she would pick up my siblings and bring them to practice. Then she would drive me home. She would take one more lap to the pool and back to my house to bring Jennifer and Jarad home at 9:00 p.m. before she went home for the night. On top of all the pickups and drop-offs, she had food prepared for each stop. It was futile for me to try to refuse food on the way from school to practice because I would then have to hear about how I needed the energy to complete the brutal workout that my coach Jim Ellis was about to deliver. One day there would be hot soup in a thermos waiting when I got in the car. Other days there would be homemade cheesesteaks. On still others there would be ramen noodles. All of it was kept warm using a hot bag and jars of boiling water. When I was finished with my meal, I could go into the trunk, which she literally turned into a mobile convenience store and snack on my choice of chips, Snickers, Blow Pops, or whatever else she had snagged from the wholesale store near our house in West Philly. Even when I was in high school and took the train from Central High School (CHS) to the pool, she would still make me a snack and deliver it as she dropped off my sister at practice. At one point the meals were a source of embarrassment because I feigned myself Mr. Cool who was too old to still have Nana cooking after-school snacks for me. On top of that my homies were masters at imitating her voice as she would call me to the car. All that embarrassment went out the window as I got older and realized that I didn't have to spend as much money on food during the week, and the practices got so hard that I really needed the food before the workouts. Soon my friends were joining me at the back of the car for something to snack on before and after practice. Nana was always more than willing to share. As far as she was concerned, my friends were additional grandchildren who needed the same energy boost that I did when it came to getting ready for practice. Her trunk was open to all.

The fact that I was spoiled set the foundation for how I would treat myself as an adult as well as how I would approach relationships and eventually my own family. My father would go without so that we could continue to enjoy the lifestyle he felt we deserved. He famously drove some of the most beat-up cars I have ever seen and rarely spent money enhancing his wardrobe. My mother did whatever she had to do to make sure that every Easter there was a new suit for me and my brother as well as a dress for my sister. There was never a Christmas where we came downstairs to an empty tree, and despite my habit of losing everything that wasn't snapped on to my body, at some point it would get replaced. When jackets made by Starter became popular in the early nineties, my mother got me one bearing the name of my favorite college basketball team, the Georgetown Hoyas. The first day I wore it, it got stolen from swim practice, and I just knew I wasn't getting it replaced. What killed me even more was that it seemed like all of my boys got Starter jackets that Christmas, and out of all the jackets that were on the rack that day, only mine was stolen. This didn't sit well with Nana, and she took me to the Gallery the very next day and bought me a new jacket. When I was in college, Nana continued to look out for me, as she would lend me her car on the weekends provided I would bring my laundry when I came to pick it up. This laundry was washed and ironed by the time I dropped the car off on Monday, and she also packed food for the week, which kept my roommates and I from having to go to campus dining as often. As an adult, the behavior of my parents and Nana stuck with me. I had it in my mind that I needed to be willing to go without so that my family could have. It also meant that I sought a partner who would be as willing to give of herself for her family as mine did for me. In addition, in looking at a potential partner's family, I wanted to see if they treated their children in a manner similar to how my parents treated me.

The strong work ethic that my parents displayed in order to make sure that the material needs of my siblings and I were met meant that there was precious little time to attend to our emotional needs and wants. Our household was not one where hugs and kisses were the norm. I felt loved because of how well my parents took care of me, but when I compared the outward expression of that love to others or what I saw on TV, it was different. I don't remember the first time I told either of my parents I loved them, but I know I was into my teens. While I would often hug Nana and other members of my extended family, I rarely exchanged hugs with my parents, which almost seemed to be by design. When I would get in trouble, which was often, my dad would talk about how he was being a tough disciplinarian now, but as I got older, our relationship would grow closer just as his had with his father. The words turned out to be prophetic as I certainly enjoy a closer relationship now with my parents than I did when I was a child, and there is not an occasion when I see them now that there is not a hug and an "I love you" exchanged. The arm's length on affection as a child, however, meant that as a single adult I sought those expressions of affection in my partner more than I might have if it had been a regular part of my upbringing. I needed a partner who wouldn't mind my need to be snuggled up under her or hold her hand or stroke her hair. (Okay, you can't stroke a girl's hair in the age of the weave, but you get my point.)

My confidence as a young man to be able to approach a girl came from my ability to excel in school. My parents made the financial sacrifice to send me to GFS, a private Quaker school in the heart of Germantown, so that there would be no question about the educational foundation I would receive. While I had my moments of silliness or mischief that would inevitably land me in hot water with my teachers, the academic part of school was not that difficult for me, so a great deal of my identity became wrapped up in my ability to do well on tests and assignments. In addition, I considered myself an athlete because of my swimming and overall fitness, so by middle school I fashioned myself somewhat of a Renaissance man. The cocoon-like environment that GFS provided only enhanced this perception.

When I left GFS after eighth grade in the spring of 1991, I was confident that I could go into any educational environment and thrive both academically and socially. I went to Central, which was a complete 180-degree turn from the environment I enjoyed at GFS. The class of '95 at GFS ended up being 72 students while my graduating class at Central was 494. Whereas GFS had a sprawling campus with multiple gyms, fields, and buildings, Central was one four-story building with facilities that could best be described as serviceable when I arrived in 1991. To its credit, the gym and science rooms were all renovated during my time there as was the library. Central is a magnet school, which means that you had to do well on a citywide test to gain acceptance. It was among a handful of schools that could lay claim to the "best school in the city" title. Central has a long tradition of producing graduates who have gone on to the most competitive universities and become successful professionals in all fields. As I anticipated, the academics, while challenging, did not kill me. My real growth came socially as I learned to navigate through a student body that brought students together from all different neighborhoods and backgrounds.

It was at Central that I really began to figure out how to connect with ladies given who I was. Lots of dudes talk about having game—in other words, the ability to use poetic lines to gain the attention and affections of one or more ladies. I had none of that. I hated rejection, so the idea of using some line I heard someone else use or approaching a young lady without knowing anything about her just wasn't comfortable for me. The successes that I had in dating in high school had to do with me developing relationships organically without any game involved. Whenever I tried to behave in a manner outside of what was natural to me or instilled in me by my parents, I inevitably had problems. I shouldn't have been surprised, given how much effort my parents put into making me understand how they believed I should comport myself as a young man.

The first time I ever got a C on a report card happened to coincide with my first girlfriend experience, and when news of that grade made it to my dad, he wasted no time sitting me down and delivering one of his famous monologues. It was tradition in my house that when you got in trouble, you had to weather the storm of my father first blowing his top at you and then the forty-five- to sixty-minute talk that followed, which was loaded with lessons about life. A C grade was not acceptable in the house, so the monologue was about how I had to be responsible and stay focused on the task at hand. At the time the tasks were to get good grades and to swim as fast as I could. There was no room for talking on the phone with some little girl. As I got older and could handle more mature topics, those got layered in as well. He talked about the responsibility of having sex and the need to use protection. He talked about the duties of fatherhood and the need to be humble and consistent. He always highlighted the types of characteristics that he wanted to see develop in me like patience, compassion, and the ability to communicate honestly. What made these lessons stick even until today is that my dad lived this life that he spent so much time talking about. He got up every day and was consistent. I saw him sacrifice for his children. He wasn't a heavy drinker, so we never saw him drunk, and even as my parents' marriage started to deteriorate, he never laid hands on my mother. It was not only my father who practiced what he preached but also many of the other men in my life.

The fathers of my teammates on the Philadelphia Department of Recreation (PDR) swim team were also an influence in that they provided additional evidence of the behavior that my dad talked about in his monologues. These were men who were professionals, but not to the point where they were not present for their children. I spent so much time with my teammates between the ages of ten to eighteen that it's fair to say that these fathers were additional surrogates for me. I got an inside look at the way they taught their sons and found that in many ways their messages were the same as my father's. I could never really think that my dad was being overly hard on me because the fathers of my best friends were preaching the same message. These men served as important role models for the ways that men go about the business of being career-oriented yet attendant to the needs of their families.

When it came to my earliest relationships, my mother made it very clear when she thought it was appropriate for me to be dating. As a sophomore in high school, my mother told me that I was too young to have a girlfriend shortly after I had gotten an upperclassman (a junior) to fill that position. Here I thought I was acting mature and behaving in a way that I had been taught to the point where an upperclassman was willing to go out with me. My mother had other ideas. Eighteen was the age for dating because at least then you could drive a date somewhere. Until then there would be no official recognition of any girlfriends as far as my mother was concerned.

My mother also made her expectations about my behavior with women clear just before I was about to start school at Penn in the summer of 1995. I had been accepted into a one-week pre-freshman program sponsored by the African-American studies department known as the AFAMS program. We took classes during the day and socialized at night with the occasional academic assignment due to keep us honest. Sometime during that week I got cozy enough with a young lady that I nearly said good-bye to my virginity. So in preparation to return to campus only a few weeks later with the hopes of sealing the deal, I had bought condoms and had them in the bag that I had taken to campus. Given that I was spoiled and never did my own laundry as a teen, my mother unpacked that bag and found the condoms. So as I prepared one night to go hang out on campus after AFAMS, she stopped me at the door and sat me down. Her message was brief and to the point, and it went something like this:

"Jonathan, sex is not something to be toyed around with," she said. "Do you understand me?"

"Yes, Mom."

"These girls are not toys, and you do not enter into a sexual relationship lightly. Do you understand me?"

"Yes, Mom," I said.

"All right."

And with that I scurried out the door. The fact that I remember that conversation like it was yesterday indicates the impact. However, I wish that she would have said all that was going through her mind that night so that I would have been better equipped for what was coming my way. I might have sidestepped some of the anguish I would later face, but that was not her way. I imagine that monologue would have gone something like: "If you're going to be having sex, then know that you have now entered the adult world, and if you're going to act like an adult, then you'd better be prepared for the adult consequences that having sex can bring. Talking all night on the phone and going to the movies with your little girlfriends won't prepare you for that. I'm your mother, and I know just how sensitive and naïve you really are. If you think you're going to that school and you're just going to have your way with these girls, you're wrong, and you're going to get your feelings hurt. Please act like you have some home training and be respectful. If you do find someone worthy of having sex with, make sure you use this protection that you bought because I'm not ready for grandchildren yet."

That speech would have made the relationship landscape clearer, and though I probably would have made some of the same mistakes, I might have made less. There is no class or video that explains to you the difference between puppy love where you're just trying to get a kiss good night and grown-up love where the physical acts are wrapped up in more complex emotions. Outside of my mother's warning, I was left to decipher much of that difference on my own through watching television or listening to the radio. When I asked my mother about that moment, she recalled it this way:

> From my perspective and memory, this is how it went when it came to dating for you and your siblings: When you were thirteen and Jennifer was ten, I had the two of you sit down to watch the video of Pastor Miles Munro. This video dealt with relationships and marriage from the Christian perspective. Yes, I wanted you guys to know that any person with whom you became involved was to be respected both emotionally and physically. And conversely, that you would demand respect.
>
> I don't remember setting a hard-and-fast rule about what age you should start dating. I knew that there were young ladies that you liked and vice versa. I knew about the phone calls—no cell phones at that time—and the love notes you were receiving. Brie, I always thought was more into you than you were into her. Madison, I never knew what happened

there. And then there was Nina. Just let me say, God gives you what you need, not necessarily what you want. And then there was Stacy. I never cared that much for her because I felt that she was just using you.

I knew that this was all a part of growing up. I did not want you to move into a serious relationship too fast, so I did not make it easy for you. Additionally there were just some things that were not going to take place in my home. Young ladies were not allowed in the house when I and/or your father were not home, and they were never to be in your room. I think you lost your virginity at Penn that summer week. As evidence of that were the scratches on your back in addition to the condoms.

In my view, at that point in your life you were older and more mature, and I needed to step back and let you find your way. As I observe the relationship you have with your wife, I wonder where you learned the give and take of married life as this was not something that you learned from your father and me. Hopefully you learned from our mistakes.

.

Learning from Cliff Huxtable

The Cosby Show was like a home study course in relationship dynamics for me growing up. We never missed an episode in our house no matter what time my brother, sister, and I had swim practice. The VCR was always set, and to this day, I would put the Carroll family collection of taped *Cosby* episodes up against anybody's. *The Cosby Show* was important enough in our household that when *The Simpsons* became popular in the early '90s and shared the same Thursday night time slot as the *Cosbys*, we were not allowed to watch *The Simpsons*. Similar to the way I learned a great deal watching how the PDR families related to each other, *The Cosby Show* was a weekly display of how families could work and, more importantly, how my parents thought a family should work. Cliff and Claire Huxtable were professional. They outwardly displayed that they loved each other and their kids. There were lessons on values and on the importance of family, education, and hard work. So in one thirty-minute episode I was getting messages on how to be a young man and brother to my siblings from Theo and then how to be a husband and father from Cliff. To this day, those images still resonate. This is not to say that I didn't understand that the show was fictional, but it helped me understand the environment my parents were trying to create in our household and the road that they wanted us to travel to adulthood. Ironically, on the show you had one daughter who went to an Ivy League school (Sandra) and two daughters (Denise and Vanessa) who went to historically Black colleges and universities (HBCUs). In the Carroll house I ended up at the Ivy League school (UPenn) while my sister and brother went to HBCUs (Howard and Lincoln respectively). Our college choices were not solely based on the immersion into the show, but it certainly helped establish an expectation of the academic excellence we were to uphold. As a grown man, I think about how Cliff Huxtable was a doctor, but he did not miss opportunities to parent his children or attend to his relationship with his wife. I have carried that image until today, and all career decisions I make are filtered through what it would mean for my ability to be a husband and parent.

The Power of Music

The music that I was exposed to when I was growing up also had an impact on the way that I understood relationships early on. Most of my music exposure happened while I was riding in the car with either of my parents. This meant the R & B soul being played on WDAS and jazz being played on WRTI. I became a fan of Stevie Wonder, Earth, Wind, and Fire, Al Green, The Whispers, and my all-time favorite, Anita Baker. I also grew to appreciate the musical skills of jazz artists like Joe Sample, Grover Washington Jr., and Kenny G.

The message that resonated with me in many of these classic R & B songs was that a love that meant something was one that was dedicated and required work, but in turn, that work would bring happiness. By the time I graduated high school, I was listening to equal parts hip-hop and R & B. I had become a fan of Big Daddy Kane and Ice Cube and groups like A Tribe Called Quest, De La Soul, KRS-One, Leaders of the New School, and Gang Starr. The message about ladies was a little different. Most MCs were talking about how many ladies they had and their exploits, but without the romance that the soul crooners were talking about. Luther Campbell, a.k.a. Luke Skyywalker, for example, had his famous Luke Dancers, and the visual of ladies dropping their ample bottoms down to the floor as soon as the music started appealed to me much more at the time than having to spend a whole lot of effort romancing a girl with the hopes that I might get a kiss good night after a date. Despite my parent's best efforts to steer my tastes one way when it came to music and television in particular, the more I listened and watched rap videos, the more I found my behavior influenced by the perceived rapper lifestyle, where women were in abundance and were willing to cater to a man's every whim and need. This created a Jekyll-and-Hyde internal struggle for me. One minute I was focused on one young lady and courting in a traditional way, and then the next minute I was acting like this classic 2 Live Crew verse, "I'm like a dog in heat, a freak without warning. I have an appetite for sex 'casuse *me so horny!*"

When I stepped onto the University of Pennsylvania campus as a college freshmen, this identity struggle would continue to play out with newfound freedom— no more parents controlling my schedule, no 7:45 a.m. church service to remind me of the consequences of unsanctified behavior. I had to learn the hard way who I really wanted to be and what was going to be acceptable for the ladies I wanted to be with.

As I reflected on the things that influenced my sense of manhood, it inspired me to ask my peers if they had role models in their youth that had had an impact on how they viewed relationships and marriage. Here's what they had to say:

Royale: I watched my dad. He's a great example of what it meant to be in a loving relationship and to care for your spouse and to provide for your family, so I think that's something that is in me to want to offer to any relationship that I've gone into.

Michael: I guess having two parents, that this year, what is this '13? This year will be thirty-nine years that they've been married. So I think... marriage isn't always peaches and cream. You're going to have your rough patches. And seeing my parents work through the various trials and tribulations kinda embeds or ingrains that in you.

O'Neil: I always knew that I didn't really want to be like my father. He was really an abrasive individual. And it's not me. It's not really my personality.

Terrence: I would say I learned a lot about what I thought I knew about relationships from just pop culture.

While having positive marriage role models does not in itself mean that one will choose to marry or when, it certainly has an impact in that it embeds in the psyche that there is a value to life being lived with a partner and that there is a benefit to living life this way as opposed to doing it alone. For Royale, Mike, and myself, having that father role model gave us a clear idea of what kind of life was possible with a good partner. For O'Neil and Terrence, they had to spend more time learning through trial and error. Thankfully they had people in their lives who helped them realize who they wanted to be as men. Once you engage in that identity work, it becomes much easier to find complementary partners with whom to associate.

Becoming a Relationship Owner

Take your time, young man

(Mama used to say).

Don't you rush to get old.

—Junior

When people hear that Nkechi and I got married at twenty-five and that we both went to Penn at the same time, they reasonably deduce that we dated in college, which draws a chuckle from both of us. We share a laugh because we know that neither of us were ready for the type of relationship we share now when we were on campus, particularly me. Despite my mother's warning, I came to campus thinking that I was going to take full advantage of the favorable ratio of women to men that I had heard about. My experience in the AFAMS program lead me to believe that this wasn't going to be that difficult as it was clear that there were plenty of women coming to campus looking to find eligible frolic partners.

Less than a week after school stared in the fall of 1995, I met a young lady named Stacy who would completely reshape everything I understood about relationships, particularly ones that were intended to have any kind of lasting future. We met after *casino night* took over Houston Hall and Bodek Lounge. Aside from the caramel skin and proportional curvatures, her green eyes (contacts) stayed with me the most. As I got to know her, her confidence, ambition, and strength of character proved to be equally attractive. Little more than introductions were exchanged that night after everyone had returned to the dorms, but when I got word that she was looking for me the next day, I wasted no time finding her to see what was up. That was the beginning of an off-and-on relationship that would last the next four years and take me through the full gamut of accompanying emotions that are involved when you are supposed to be seriously committed to someone. That relationship showed me that I wasn't ready to handle that responsibility. There are a number of lessons that I still use to this day that I took from the debris.

Be Clear in What You Want

Having just lost my virginity, my nose was wide open when I was inevitably posed the following questions: "So what are we doing? Where do you see this going? Are you trying to be serious?" I was still getting used to the fact that I could have a girl sleep over and not have to worry about my parents, so I said what I thought needed to be said for my ability to play house to continue. "I'm trying to be serious. I'm not about playing games."

That put a nice bow tie on that convo, and I remember actually being proud because here I was, acting like my mother had told me to act if I was going to have sex. I had only been at school two weeks and here I was set to bring somebody home to meet the family. Unfortunately I had no idea what "I'm trying to be serious" really meant. Stacy had played house before. She had gone to boarding school, so the independence that comes as a young person away from home on a coed campus wasn't new. I just knew it was what I was supposed to say and figured it couldn't be that hard to be serious with someone who had so many things working in her favor.

In hindsight, I should have been able to say something like, "Look, we just got on campus. I'm feelin' you and definitely want to get to know you better, but I'm not ready to be anybody's husband yet."

At eighteen I wasn't that mature. All I could see was that I wanted to protect my chance of more loving with this young woman, so I tried to play grown-up and got burned. In addition, the dating culture at Penn wasn't at all about monogamy. As Stacy reflected,

> "The interesting dynamic at Penn played a major role in why this lasted so long. The trend was that anything lasting more than a semester was perceived as being a public full-on relationship that signified true commitment and maturity, while the truth was that privately many folks in the "admirable" long-term relationships were a hot mess privately. Everybody knew, but everyone still respected the public "wifey" or "hubby" because that was the culture at Penn due to the ratio of seven women to one man."

While it would have been easy to continue conforming to the relationship culture at Penn, who knows what Stacy's response would have been had I answered the questions with the type of raw honesty that is necessary for the relationship-direction conversation to be productive. If she had said, "I'm not on that wavelength," then we would have parted ways and moved on. If she said, "All right, I hear where you're coming from. If we're going get to know each other, that means we start from square one without the frolicking," then I could've made an informed choice. This isn't the way it went down, and I ended up making mistake after mistake because I wasn't willing to do the work of communicating honestly that would get me the reward I wanted, more frolic time.

"You're Not a Player. You Mess Up a Lot."

My first attempt at playing house ended after one semester when Stacy and I parted ways for the first time. I went home, tail between my legs because I hadn't been able to be the grown-up I thought I was supposed to be at eighteen. Nor had I acted in the way my parents had raised me. I was resilient, however, and over that winter break I started hanging with a girl I'd dated during my senior year in high school who was now a senior herself. Next thing I know, I'm having another conversation about whether or not I'm trying to be serious, and with my understanding that the chances of frolicking with a girl were limited if they thought you were just trying to "hit and run," I of course said, "I'm trying to be with you. I don't want to play games."

Games, however, were exactly what I started to play. When Nina graduated that spring and went off to school sixteen hours away, I returned to campus for my sophomore year and almost immediately started messing around with Stacy again. Stacy knew about Nina, and she even witnessed many a morning phone call with her, as Nina called almost daily from school; however, she was fine being my campus frolic partner, so I took full advantage of the situation. The problem for me was that once I found I could have one frolic partner, I started to think it would be okay if I had another, and soon I found myself in situations where I was calling people the wrong name and people were starting to call me out for the love triangle I was involved in. I hit rock bottom when it got to the point where there was actually an altercation between Stacy and another young lady I was messing with, all while my "girlfriend" was away at college. To be clear, the confrontation had less to do with me directly as it did with Stacy feeling betrayed by someone she had befriended who had now crossed the line. As she put it, "It was about me letting her know that it was the ultimate rule-breaker. Don't shit where you eat. You were free to do what you wanted to do, but she crossed the line personally with me."

My poor attempt at being pimp of the year should have opened my eyes that this wasn't behavior that I could make work. I wasn't being honest. I knew I hadn't been raised this way, and at the end of the day the ends didn't justify the means. Unfortunately the Jekyll-and-Hyde struggle continued inside me, so it wasn't until I graduated that I was secure enough in who I was to truly leave the games behind. This was such a critical time of growth for me as far as relationships that I went and asked Stacy for her input so that the picture could be as clear as possible. She recalled the time this way:

> I'm stubborn as heck and see myself as a prize on many levels, so when you came back [to school] with Nina, I didn't take her seriously at all. I saw it as a reaction to me moving on after you and I broke up the first time. So me being okay with it was not really that I was okay with the fact you were in a new relationship. It was that I wouldn't acknowledge it. And I actually wanted to be in a relationship with

you at that time. (Which is why I broke up with someone who had just proposed to me. I definitely didn't communicate that. Tony is a great guy. I was just way too young for that level of commitment so that proposal had the opposite effect of the intent—just scared the crap out of me and pushed me right back to something that I was more comfortable with at my age, which was the relationship with you. I knew Tony would see it through for the four years until I graduated so that we could get married afterwards, and I wasn't ready for the rest of my life yet.) That's pivotal to the story because I was now in my own long-term relationship, trying to see if I could walk out the ultimate level of commitment at seventeen, but couldn't let go of you either.

Funny how more than a decade has past since the Stacy era, and I had never heard about the proposal until I touched base with her to get her blessing on what I had written. It just goes to show the shaky ground that two young people were trying to build a relationship on without really understanding what that would mean. For my part I misunderstood the value of friendship and communication. It's not like my parents didn't try to explain these things to me, but hard head that I am, I had to experience it for myself and face all the emotional angst that comes with trying to proceed in relationships without being completely upfront and honest about my intentions. Members of my panel had similar growing pains while they were dating.

Royale: I found that there were parts of me that just wanted to sleep with women and then those women, that's not what they wanted, but they would mask that so as to not chase me off. I was like, 'Oh, okay, I thought we were having fun,' but it was like no, people have feelings, they're interested in you, they want to pursue something more with you. As a typical guy you try to ignore that part, but what you're doing is you're not being completely honest with them about what this transaction is. There's no reciprocation. It's one-sided in many ways. So that's the thing that I've taken out of dating is be more aware of what the other person's feelings are and try to be more respectful of their feelings.

O'Neil: I think I always related to people, especially early on with my partners as more on a friendship level. We'd be great friends, and the relationship part would be there as well. But it wasn't always necessarily the focus because I don't even know that I was necessarily as good at it.

Terrence: I would say the first [relationship] experience in college helped me to understand or first realize that I, in terms of dealing with women, definitely didn't have that sensitivity that you had to have in terms of understanding and validating other people's feelings and recognizing that men and women actually think differently and respond to the same things differently.

Be Yourself, Whoever That Is

I learned in college to be comfortable in my own skin and that my natural personality was enough to make me attractive to women. I didn't have to put on a persona. As a freshman, I became a proud member of the Delta Eta chapter of Kappa Alpha Psi Fraternity, Inc. (KAψ), a traditionally Black Greek Letter Organization (BGLO). The reputation of a Kappa man among other things is that he's a smooth pretty boy, and I definitely spent time in college figuring out what this meant for me. Being a member of a BGLO puts you into a whole new community

35

of people who share similar commitments to scholarship, service, and partying, or should I say "fellowship." It also meant that I could go to almost any campus and have instant connections because of my fraternal bonds. I took full advantage of those opportunities, and Cheyney, Lincoln, West Chester, Temple, and Drexel universities all became frequent party destinations. This time spent with my fraternal brethren sped up my learning curve on how I wanted to be perceived as a man and reinforced my beliefs about what was appropriate behavior around women.

Our chapter annually hosted a party during the Penn Relays weekend, one of the largest gatherings of Black fraternity and sorority members that I have ever seen, rivaled only by the Kappa Luau hosted by Florida A&M in Tallahassee, Florida. Penn Relays is the oldest and largest track meet in America, with a total attendance of more than one hundred thousand for the week that it takes place. Participating in an event like this gave me a front row seat, as brothers from all over would come to town to see who they could get with over the weekend. Some brothers were "volume shooters" when it came to hitting on women, meaning that they were like the basketball player with no conscience who kept shooting until they finally scored. Others were more efficient with their game, focusing in on only a few choice partners. I realized that I was okay with studying the prospects as best as I could before making any moves and that I didn't need to rely on the Greek paraphernalia I wore to represent my persona. If you come to Greek life as a somewhat nerdy mama's boy, then you will continue to be that after you are initiated.

Fraternity life also served as a maturity vehicle for me because in conducting the business of the frat, I developed relationships with great men of integrity who would talk about and model what it was to be a successful man who achieved both professionally and personally. Our chapter was lucky enough to have advisors that took a sincere interest in not only keeping our chapter on the straight and narrow but also in our development as young men.

These mentor relationships I developed foreshadowed the next steps in my progression as a man after I had spent more of my time in college planning parties than community programs.

While fraternity life dominated much of my undergraduate experience, a great deal of my time was spent with a small group of friends who had become my roommates by the time we were juniors. Each roommate had had a relationship that lasted multiple years, which meant a lot of time spent together as couples. The crew ultimately dubbed ourselves the "Vortex" because of how strong the bonds became between us. It seemed that once you were involved, you could never break away, even though at points the group would have been better served had some bonds been broken.

The amount of time that my roommates and I spent with each other's respective girlfriends hanging in the dorm or at social events meant that deep friendships developed to the point where the ending of my relationship with Stacy did not mean that her friendship with Mike, O'Neil, or Terrence was over. It just meant that when she would visit our dorm or later our apartment, I wouldn't be the reason. It also meant that an ex could be invited to hang with the crew and you just had to suck it up because she was friendly with everybody else. It got to the point where there were girls who had messed around with more than one of my roommates, but based on who she was friendly with in the crew, she might still hang out with us on a consistent basis. Somehow we made this all work even after our time at Penn was done.

When I talk about this web of college friendships that I had with those who have subsequently become part of my circle, there is often disbelief that such a messy set of circumstances could yield friendships that persist until today. It prompted me to ask my roommates how they characterize those times now that they can look back almost twenty years ago to the time when they started.

O'Neil: So I say that [those conversations] definitely shaped my opinion and shaped my view on relationships. Those conversations really offered insight into relationships as well.

Mike: At its core, our friendships were much bigger than the vortex. I think that is evidenced by the friendships that we still have today... I think that the feeling of looking out for the females in the vortex derived from the strength of the friendships that were established, before the vortex was created.

Terrence: Having people around you that support your relationships was big. You know being in a relationship, it's tough when you're around people that don't support you. When they're saying, "Ah, yeah, you don't need to be with him. You don't need to be with her," or something like that. That was rough, but when your friends, your significant others, everybody gets along, it makes it a lot easier.

There was very little spread geographically once we all graduated and started working, so it was nothing for us to burn up I-95 to see each other on a random weekend to hang out. We moved each other into our first apartments for the hefty price of a meal at the nearest International House of Pancakes (IHOP). We got puzzled looks when we would all go club together and stick together as if we were all coupled up when in fact none of us were. I thoroughly enjoyed our time hanging out and have lasting memories. However, at the time, the Vortex did more to hamper my progression toward being in the type of relationship that would lead to marriage than to help it.

It's difficult to get to know people well enough to have relationships with them when the welfare of your female friends takes time away from that effort. Furthermore, it's difficult to find a woman worth going down the relationship path with when you are preoccupied with the group dynamics within your circle of friends. For these reasons, the Vortex was both a blessing and a curse when it came to my development into someone who was ready to be a relationship owner. The curse was that while I had strong friend connections to everyone in the crew, maintaining those bonds while starting a career left little time to think about or pursue what I was looking for in a partner. I remember one particular night we went to a place called Choices in Baltimore, and eight of us stayed in the center of the dance floor in a huddle all night. Dudes would approach the ladies, and if they gave us a certain look, we knew not to go too far. The blessing was that spending that time being a friend to the ladies in the crew better prepared me to communicate when I did find someone with whom I wanted to build a life. I also learned to understand the boundaries that one must respect in order to maintain a friendship with the fairer sex.

There was always a fair amount of sexual tension in the air when we would hang, given that there had been episodes between ladies and gents in the crew. Over the years our relationships developed to the point where the friendship became more important than making things awkward with a night of physical friskiness, but that progression didn't happen without some uncomfortable moments along the way.

During my senior year of college I became really close with my friend Rachel. She didn't enter the Vortex as a roommate's girlfriend, but instead we really started to hang as senior week festivities were taking place prior to graduation. After graduation we would hang out whenever she came into town, and we would touch base on the phone and talk about everything from our struggles with relationships to our shared profession of education. After six months neither of us was dating anybody seriously, and I started to think, *What if I pushed this to be more serious? Could it work?* Never mind that she was teaching in Boston, and I was still in Philly.

One weekend when she was in town visiting, I decided to start sending signals beyond the friend wavelength and see if my feelings were reciprocated. During one conversation she mentioned liking only white gummy bears, so I made sure to leave some out for her when she came back to the apartment after she had hung out with her girlfriends one night. That earned me some cool points, but when I tried to promote myself from the futon, where I normally slept when she visited, into the extra-long twin bed where she slept, that's when Rachel put me back in the friend zone. Entry into the bed was successful as was transitioning into the spooning position. I even got a kiss, and just before we went to the point of no return by removing clothing, the proverbial record scratched to a halt. I love Rachel for how gently she communicated that she wasn't feeling me like that and that she valued me as a friend, which was something worth preserving. The genius of Rachel is that she conveyed this message with this simple question: "Don't you have an early wake-up call in the a.m.?" That was it. Ten to fifteen minutes of conversation wrapped up in eleven words. We were good enough friends for me to understand, and we remain good friends to this day as evidenced by her writing the foreword to this book. When I asked for an accuracy check in recounting the episode, she recalled,

I don't know if it was a "not feeling you like that" and more of a "this would have to be serious if we went there and I don't know if my feelings are where they'd need to be in order to commit to that." The idea of a meaningless fling was not an option, in my opinion, as that would taint the friendship in the long run. And you just weren't a meaningless fling kind of guy.

As time went on, I became more and more grateful that Rachel and I had a real friendship and did not try to make it something else. The friendship enabled me to develop further into a man who could be a good husband because of the unique ways that we interacted.

Having close female friends in the crew meant that the gents received constant affirmation that we were somehow different than many of the dudes the ladies were dating. Subconsciously there was always the reminder that we were husband material because of how we comported ourselves. We also got to pick apart the decisions that dudes were making when they were dating the ladies and take shots when we felt they didn't measure up. In one instance, I told Rachel that she was "reaching" when it came to a dude that she had brought to an event. After I met him and watched how he interacted with her, I could tell it wasn't a good fit, and based on our friendship, I had no problem telling her. It was interesting to find that the ladies didn't feel that they had the same license to share their thoughts about the ladies we were dating.

It was never discussed between them, but the ladies never took shots at the women the gents were dating in the manner that we dissected their dates. Rachel speculated as to the reason why. "In the end, love is going to trump friendship, so if we didn't insure that the two could exist harmoniously, we'd be on the curb." The perspective is interesting because, the way I saw it, if a franchise player came into the picture, she'd have no problem blending with the people I saw as true friends. Choosing between the two was never an issue, and that's exactly what happened.

By the time I graduated college, I had figured out the most important characteristics in my future partner, and I had become resolute that I wasn't going to settle for a role player, someone who could do one thing especially well like cook, perform between the sheets, or make lots of money in her profession but ultimately didn't have the full package. The franchise player recipe that I kept in my head read as follows (with no particular order to the qualities):

1. *Height*—I dated a number of "shorties" during college, and after a while I got tired of how that dynamic worked physically. When I'm six feet one and my girlfriend is five feet one, that means lots of bending over for hugs. When you bend at the waist for a hug, your ass sticks out, so you don't really get that close body contact that you want from somebody who's more than a friend. So then you end up lifting your partner, which is awkward considering that this is a grown person and not a child. When you lay down together, of course all of these issues are nullified, but that's only a percentage of the time. I always wonder how it works with the incredibly tall athletes I see with wives who are barely five feet tall. By the end of college I was in the market for a woman on the upper end of the height spectrum.

2. *"We Are One" Attitude*—There's a line in the chorus of Frankie Beverly's great song that goes,

"No matter what we do/We are One/Love will see us through/We are One." My father had been instilling this philosophy of oneness in my head since I was of dating age. He would constantly tell me that I needed to find a woman "who's going to be in your corner." The meaning I took from the gospels of John Carroll and Frankie Beverly was that my franchise player had to be in it with me until the end, good times and bad, sickness and health, all the stuff that gets pledged at the altar on your wedding day. I needed someone who would roll with me if I decided to leave a six-figure job to go teach water safety to kids in Belize or sell paintings on the street in Rome. There is a certain confidence that is awakened in a man when he knows that the woman he loves has his back unconditionally and is willing to sacrifice in order to help him reach his full potential.

3. *Ambition*—Much like a franchise player in athletics has a unique self-confidence and knows that at any moment he or she can put the team on his or her back and get stuff done, I wanted a partner with such confidence in her abilities to

do whatever she chose professionally and not be totally dependent on somebody doing something for her. In complement, I wanted someone who was passionate about everything she did and was secure enough to let her emotions show and not hide them behind a poker face.

4. *Strong Family Ideals*—I knew I wanted to have a family, and I desired a partner who would share the commitment to building a strong family. I wasn't so much concerned that my partner come from some idyllic household, as I've never met a person who doesn't have a little dysfunction in their family. What was more important was how that family experience was processed and how it impacted my partner's philosophy. For example, I knew as a parent, I didn't want to rely on fear as a primary method of keeping my children in line. I remembered that my healthy fear of my father's anger growing up often made me try to lie my way out of trouble first instead of telling the truth. I wanted a partner who looked at family similarly.

5. *Matching Belief Principles*—I was raised in a Baptist church. For as long as I can remember, my

father was a deacon. When I would get in trouble and receive one of his infamous monologues, his favorite religious saying was always part of the text. "There, but for the grace of God go I." So while I have struggled with my faith over the years, I have always subscribed to the belief system that God is my savior, and I needed a partner who had a similar belief system. The Bible says, "Do not be yoked together with unbelievers. For what do righteousness and wickedness have in common? Or what fellowship can light have with darkness?" (2 Corinthians 6:14 NIV). In plain terms, a marriage between a person who grew up Jewish and one who grew up Muslim, for example, could work, but there could be issues when it comes to how to raise children. I felt it was important to be in lockstep with my partner on this so that when it came to feeding our relationship and building our family, there would be no confusion as to the way faith would be viewed and utilized.

It's funny to me now as a married man to think that I really had a list of things that I felt would constitute my perfect partner, particularly the physical component because at the end of the day what draws me most to Nkechi is how she embraces the "we are one" attitude. She has been in my corner from the beginning, riding shotgun and giving instructions since 2000. Having that is way more important than the fact that she is nearly six feet in height. Alimi spoke very passionately to this point as well about what is truly important in finding a partner.

> The thing you really want in a mate that doesn't always show up on a spreadsheet, [is] someone that even when they're angry, they're never spiteful. They fight nice when they're mad with you. You know, a person who doesn't kick you when you're down. These are the things that someone should be looking for. Now [Dahn] she's college-educated, she reads twice as fast, all of that good stuff. You know she's gorgeous, she's a super workout fanatic, she's pretty, she's sexy, all the things I like, you know? I like 'em brown with round parts, she's brown she's got round parts, which works for me, you know all of these other things that were great. But they're not what's gonna keep. They're not

going to keep you when it gets hard, and you're

going to be tested.

While I felt a sense of accomplishment in having figured out what it was that I wanted in a franchise player, there was a great deal of frustration that built when I could not find that woman right away. I felt like I had matured to the point where I could support this type of woman and be a desirable husband. What I quickly learned was that even if a woman has franchise player qualities, she has to be ready to step into that role. Kobe Bryant and Kevin Garnett, for example, both showed skills on the basketball court that led to both of them being drafted out of high school. They had franchise player written all over them as far as the Los Angeles Lakers and Minnesota Timberwolves were concerned, but it took a few years before they were really able to take the torch and run with it. I had to learn to measure a woman's seriousness in addition to checking off my list of qualities in order to protect against getting my heart stomped on. While I felt like I had developed to a point where I could carry on this type of relationship, I had not yet grasped just how much commitment it would take to make such a partnership thrive.

You Gotta Lose First to Win

Because of you, feelings I handle with care.
Some niggaz recognize the light, but they can't
handle the glare.

—Common

The last serious relationship I had before I met Nkechi started just as I was about to graduate from college. She was a year older than me and a great girl. She filled every box I had on my wish list. On a number of levels we connected, and the relationship developed very quickly. Most of my social time my final weeks as an undergrad was spent with her. I met and spent time with her family. I gave a swim lesson to her nephew and spent a weekend in Virginia Beach with her after graduation. Everything was moving along, and then I decided that I had to trample boundaries. I visited a past frolic partner, and killed any chances I had of making my relationship work by sleeping with her. Somehow I rationalized that one last moment with a girl I enjoyed having sex with would have no bearing on the grown-up relationship I was trying to have. I was an idiot. I came home from that weekend, and the relationship was never the same. I was hurt when I got dumped because I knew I had let a good woman get away. It was a clear wake-up call that if in fact I was going to be with a woman of the caliber I desired, then I had to be fully prepared to act in kind. I needed to develop a discipline and practice a level of communication that would demonstrate to potential franchise players that I was serious with not only my words but also my actions.

Nkechi was prone to having longtime boyfriends even in college. Had we dated during those years, I likely would have messed it up because I was still learning the type of commitment it took to be with a franchise player. It wasn't until we were both out of school and pursuing careers that we started talking, and even then it almost didn't happen.

A mutual friend of ours, the talented Rob Murat, was performing at Soul Cafe in New York. My roommates and I drove up from Philly to support him. As a side note, his opening act that night was another Penn alum named John Stephens, who later became John Legend and has had a pretty good career. As my roommates and I were waiting to be seated, Nkechi strolled in, and everything stopped as far as I was concerned. She was rocking gold streaks in the hair, a formfitting baby blue top, nice jeans, and a leather jacket. There had been previous double-take experiences when she walked into the room, but this was one of the first where I was not with someone else. My goal immediately became to at least get her number and find out if she was with someone.

At this time in my life I was working as a second-grade assistant teacher, a job that I loved but paid peanuts. Impressing women with my earning potential was never going to be my approach. However, the fact that I was an elementary teacher always seemed to be a conversation starter. Without fail, any time I would explain that I was working with second-graders, women would inevitably respond, "Aw," and the conversation would build from there. The funny thing is that I never intended for my job to be a pickup line; however, on this night I hoped it would at least extend the conversation, and it did. After

I listened to Nkechi describe how she participated in weekly conference calls with Alan Greenspan to keep the economic world spinning as part of her job at the New York Federal Reserve, she asked what I was up to, and I hit her with the line. I remember elbowing Mike, who was standing nearby as he had heard this reaction more than once. The rest of the conversation was pretty much a blur until we got to the topic of who we were both seeing. I remember saying that I wasn't seeing anyone and hoping that Nkechi would respond in kind that there wasn't anyone serious on her radar either. Instead she replied that she had *friends*, which I took to mean that she was juggling a roster of dudes. I wasn't trying to be part of anybody's roster, so in my mind, I was content having had the conversation and letting Nkechi get to her blind date. Thankfully for me, that date didn't go so well.

Soon after the friends comment, my roommates and I got our table, where we enjoyed the show. As far as I knew, Nkechi was off enjoying her date. I was surprised to see her stop by our table on her way out the door to say bye and more surprised when she asked for my number. Of course I gave it to her, but when I saw that she was neither writing it down nor putting it in her phone, I thought, *I'll never hear from her.* As she later admitted, she forgot the number as soon as she turned to walk away from the table. I also later found out that the reason she had stopped by the table on her way out was that her date had ended quickly and a visit to our table was part of her escape route. She had selected Rob's event because she knew that if the date didn't go well, she would at least have familiar faces around to retreat to. As it turned out, the date went sideways when she asked dude what he liked to do, and he replied, "I like to *fuck*!" "And scene!" as they say in Hollywood. When Nkechi decided that it was time to go, she refused to let the dude drive her home, leaving her to have to walk to the train alone in the rain. Had I known this, I certainly would have taken her home. Instead she rolled out, and I continued to enjoy Rob's performance with the fellas. In my mind, Nkechi was still a franchise player, but we just weren't on the same page for a relationship to work... yet.

Thankfully during senior week I put my contact information in a book one of my classmates was passing around. After she forgot my number, Nkechi contacted our mutual friend because sometime during our conversation at Soul Café I had mentioned seeing her recently. Nkechi got my e-mail address and sent me a note saying that it was good to see me and thanked me for "bailing her out" of her blind date. She ended the e-mail by saying that we should stay in touch. I took this as my chance to get to the top of her friends list. She left her cell number in the e-mail, so I called her. I wasn't about to let a franchise player get away without putting in my best offer. That first conversation lasted three hours. We talked about our families, our careers, what we liked, what we disliked. We talked daily after that, and after she made one particular visit to Philly, I knew that we had a future.

As a student, Penn Relays weekend was like a holiday on my calendar. It meant watching some of the best track in the world on Friday and Saturday, and then the annual fraternity/sorority step show and after-party Saturday night. Even after graduating and hanging up my Kappa kane, Penn Relays weekend meant seeing friends who were no longer on the yard, a Greek homecoming of sorts. On that Saturday the residential area on Penn's campus, known as Superblock, went from a normally quiet plaza notorious for being a wind tunnel to a gathering place for members of BGLOs young and old. The day was spent reminiscing, singing fraternity and sorority songs, networking, and politicking. My day would start at the track with my roommates, and it would end with a visit to Superblock before I headed to the step show. In the spring of 2000 I wasn't really dying to go to the step show or do Superblock after I had participated in the step show for the past four years. I was also working, so my weekends had become more about resting than partying. I did, however, ask Nkechi to come down so we could hang and spend some quality time together. She didn't say no, but she didn't leave the impression that she was going to make the trip. She wasn't a track fan. Nor was she in a sorority, so Penn Relays weekend didn't hold the same appeal that it did for me. Not a problem as far as I was concerned. Just meant that I could enjoy the meet without having to worry about entertaining, and that's what I did. The races and female scenery were great as always, and at the end of the meet my roommates and I dispersed to pursue our separate social agendas.

After I secured my pass to the step show, I started making my way toward Superblock to see who was still hanging out before the show started and get a sense of what had happened while I was at the track. Unbeknownst to me, O'Neil had run into Nkechi. She had decided to come down after all. The way the story was later told, after a bit of small talk O'Neil asked Nkechi, "Does Jon know you're here?" to which she replied in the negative; however, something in the way O'Neil asked the question gave Nkechi the impression that I'd be happy to see her, so she posted up in Superblock with her wing mates and hung out, waiting to see if I eventually strolled that way. I exchanged a few fraternal handshakes and man hugs before I saw her, and when I did, I paused before I walked over to the bench where she was sitting. The reason? There was a dude with a dog sitting next to her. My initial thought, *She brought a dude to Relays?* Then I thought, *This* has *to be a friend, or else I would've heard about him over these last few weeks that we've been talking daily.* When I got to the bench, Nkechi introduced me to the dude with the dog, who seemed unimpressed by the whole Superblock scene. He turned out to be her good friend and MIA wingman. The night of Rob Murat's show at Soul Café, he fell asleep and failed to show up as the escape hatch in case the date went badly. To make up for his poor wingman behavior, he got to ride shotgun to Philly. In addition to Tim, Nkechi's friend Yma tagged along for the ride. The four of us shot the breeze for a little bit before it was time for them to get back on the road up the New Jersey Turnpike.

Before they departed I did manage to get Nkechi away from her crew to thank her for coming down and let her know that I hoped we would get to hang again soon. She replied that she'd like that, and I gave her a hug. A good one. Not the kind you give a friend where your ass sticks out so you don't seem too intimate. This was a solid embrace. As we separated, I said something corny about needing more hugs like that in my life. She smiled, said something like, "That can be arranged," and then gave me a quick peck on the lips. Totally caught me off guard. The only thing I could come up with to say was, "Thank you." For that brief period of the hug and the kiss, I had forgotten that I was in the middle of Superblock with hundreds of people, not to mention two of her close friends sitting close by, but that awareness returned as soon as the kiss happened. I told her to give me a call when she got in, and I got out of Superblock as fast as I could before someone I knew called attention to what had just happened. I didn't even look in the direction of where Nkechi's crew had been sitting, as I assumed they had watched the whole thing unfold.

My assumption was ultimately wrong, as neither had seen the first public display of affection Nkechi and I shared. When they left Superblock, Nkechi and Co. stopped for pizza before they headed up I-95. It was over pizza that Nkechi relayed that she had kissed me, which surprised neither of them. It did set the stage for Tim, the dog-wielding wingman, to take credit for our eventual marriage. Had there been no guilt for not doing his job at Soul Café, he would not have come down the Turnpike. The whole course of events may have been different. That kiss stayed on my mind as I watched my frat brothers win the step show and was a major factor in my decision to go home afterward instead of to the after-party. I wanted to talk to her to find out why she had done it. What did this kiss mean for her and us? If I was going to be burning up the highway to try to make this work, I needed to know I wasn't part of some game. When I did get her on the phone, our three-hour conversation put all those concerns to bed. This was something serious, and I didn't have to worry that Nkechi was running some game or that I was going to have to compete for playing time with the other dudes on her roster. We talked mostly about family and how important it was to both of us. Soon after Relays weekend I would begin to meet the Okoro clan.

Scouting and Drafting

Me and your daughter got a special thing going on.

You say it's puppy love. We say it's full grown.

—Andre 3000

The first member of the Okoro family I met was Nkechi's brother, Okey. It was an awkward introduction, but it told me a lot about who he is as a big brother. The first time I visited Nkechi at the apartment she shared with Okey in Queens, I had just driven from Florida, and as soon as I got to my car, I got back on the freeway and started heading north. I got lost making my way to Queens, and I finally got to the apartment around 1:00 a.m. After I greeted Nkechi at the door with another solid embrace, I was introduced to Okey. He asked how I was doing, made a joke about me getting lost, and then retired to his room for the night. No grilling me about coming into his house at 1:00 a.m. No questions about where I thought I was sleeping or how long I was staying. He let his sister be a grown-up and went about his business. In the years since, he continues to be a man of few words, even though I'm told he does a mean Michael Jackson. He's a model of responsibility because he has effectively been the man of the house for a long time. When Nkechi's father, who had not been around for a long time, became ill and later passed, Okey traveled to Nigeria with Mama Okoro to sort out his father's affairs. He works hard but always makes time for his family. Without saying much, he made it clear how his sister was to be treated. I am forever appreciative that Okey was cool during that first meeting. That encounter made getting to know the rest of the family much easier.

Nkechi's family is unique because of the kinship structure that it is built upon. While some of us grow up with family friends whom we might call uncle or aunt, the distinction about who is family and who is not is clear. This was not the case in the Nigerian-based Okoro family. Family members who were not blood related were always around at every gathering to the point where the distinctions between the families was blurry. It became routine for me to ask Nkechi if Uncle So-and-so and

Aunty What's-her-name were blood or not. The Kalu family is a shining example of this, and when I met them in the summer of 2000, it was a true immersion into the way Nigerian-based kinship ties work.

Auntie Nkacha was a very close friend of Nkechi's mother, Enuma, throughout their formative years. I met Auntie Nkacha and her husband, Uncle KMK, at their Old Westbuy, New York, home during a celebration of Auntie's leukemia going into remission. She had not yet regained all of her strength, so she greeted guests from the couch in her living room. As I sat down to exchange pleasantries, I was awed by her regal presence. She was very gracious and made it clear that I was not to play games with Nkechi. I assured her I had no plans of doing so, and my audience with her ended. Next it was time to meet her daughters, Afo, and Ogori, who were like sisters to Nkechi. If you can imagine Cinderella's stepsisters actually being protective of her instead of being haters, that's Afo and Ogori. Immediately upon meeting them, I was given a thorough once-over and put through the ringer, answering questions about my intentions with their cousin. Apparently I was the first boyfriend to be introduced to the family, so I needed to prove I was worth the honor. The rest of the afternoon was spent arguing, debating, and laughing about the current events of the time, as Afo lives to stir the pot and engage in verbal sparring. One day she will have her own show. She recalled that first meeting in the following way:

> My immediate impression was that you seemed like a "cool person"—laid-back, great sense of humor, and attractive. I recall that I noticed that Nkechi seemed very "natural" or comfortable, and to me this was a good sign. My "concern" was that since you are African-American, you may not be comfortable traveling to Nigeria, and by extension, having your future kids have a deeper exposure to Nkechi's cultural heritage.

Ironic to me that Afo's main concern at the time was my willingness to experience the Nigerian-based part of Nkechi's family when the family kinship connections were one of the things that made me feel welcome. As we were saying our good-byes that day, Afo looked at me and said, "So you really are trying to be in the family, huh?"

I answered with something to this effect: "Why wouldn't I be? Who wouldn't want to be a part of all this?" I was only half-joking. In one afternoon I really did feel like I was part of the family. Even though Nkechi and I had only been seeing each other for a couple of months, I knew that it was serious because of the way our conversations had gone. There was no pretense and no game playing. If I wanted to know something, I asked, and she answered. The same was also true for when she had questions. I had enjoyed meeting and interacting with her extended family, so it was easy to imagine myself becoming a permanent fixture at these events. It turned out that meeting the Kalus was an excellent primer for meeting the most important member of the Okoro clan.

As you begin to learn more about your partner, do not forget to make an assessment of the relationship that person has with their family. It is not an inconsequential thing. Think of a free agent in basketball who is pursued by a number of teams. One of the things that will happen (if he's smart) is that he will look at the quality of the organizations and decide which is best equipped to meet his needs. The same is true in relationships. Once you are married, it is about you and your partner and the unit you are trying to build. If your partner relies too heavily on his or her family to make decisions, then you may have problems on your hands. Whether or not they come from a stable family is not the main issue. It is whether they can use their familial experience to move forward with you. Coming from a family where marriages have been successful helps because at least the person has a notion of how to build with you. Many of the guys I interviewed talked about how their wives' families made them feel in the beginning.

Mike talking about Kelci's family: It was always clear, you know he's [Kelci's father] a reverend. So it was clear that the church is important. Doing things the right way. [He wanted] Somebody [who was] going to treat her right, take care of her.

Royale talking about April's family: Her grandmother and grandfather were a very solid couple. I looked at them and it made me hopeful. It really made me hopeful how her grandfather and her grandmother cared for each other all those many years later. Her grandmother still cooked for her grandfather. I could look at her grandfather who was eighty-something years old and see the young man in him that went out every day to work to take care of his wife.

Alimi talking about Dahn's family: I met her family, and they looked so polished to me. And they welcomed me with open arms. From the first time I met them, they were sweet. You know she's [from] a southern family very you know like former Civil Rights Movement people… Her family is literally former Civil Rights people. So there's that Morehouse, that Spelman, that college that Tuskegee feeling to it and I love that. My mom was a Black Militant, but my aunts were not. They're traditional Baptists. So her family reminded me of my aunties. I felt at home with her people immediately.

In the summer of 2000 I met Nkechi's mother, Enuma Okoro, when she came into town from the Ivory Coast, where she was living at the time. Similar to meeting Auntie Nkacha, it felt like I was meeting the queen. Picture Madge Sinclair as Queen Aoleon in *Coming to America*. That was the presence of Mama Okoro. The few times that I was in a situation to meet a girlfriend's parents, I never felt intimidated. I wasn't a criminal. Nor was I someone who looked to be disrespectful to adults. In my head meeting a girlfriend's mother was like meeting my mother. If you rubbed my mother the wrong way and didn't show proper deference, you got the cold shoulder, and it could be frostbite cold. When meeting a dad, I pictured the relationship between my father and sister. If you disrespect my sister, John Carroll will come for you, and you don't want that. This approach never failed, so I had no worries meeting Mama Okoro. As long as I was willing to carry her luggage, fetch her a drink, and eat the food she cooked, then there were no issues. As things became more serious between Nkechi and I, and it became clearer to her that we may in fact get married, she made it clear to me the dating rules she expected us to abide by.

In the summer of 2001 Mama Okoro let me know her position on the relationship Nkechi and I had while I was visiting the Ivory Coast as Nkechi's arm candy for a wedding. It was my first trip to the motherland, and while I was excited to see everything, taste the food, and soak up the history, it became clear that Mama Okoro had other plans in mind so that I would understand how much power she could wield. The first of these events occurred when I went with her to get money exchanged from American dollars to francs. We were driving around downtown, and then we started to make turns that took us off the beaten path. The whole time I was thinking, *Where's the bank? This doesn't look like an area of commerce?* I sat silently as Mama Okoro drove. She seemed to know where she was going. As we entered one street that was barely wider than an alley, Mama Okoro started to slow down as all these dudes started to jump out into the middle of the street and crowd around the car. Now I was thinking, *Are we about to get carjacked? What can I grab in this car if I need to start swinging?* Turned out that the dudes in the street were "independent currency exchange brokers" all bidding for Mama Okoro's business. The dudes were so aggressive that Mama Okoro barely cracked the window to exchange money and talk with the dude who ultimately won the bid. I don't speak French, so I had no idea what was going on. As we drove away, I know Mama Okoro was laughing at me in her head because the look on my face had to say that I had been shaken by what had just happened. That thought got confirmed when we got back to her condo and I told Nkechi the story. To this day, Mama Okoro laughs when I explain that she was out to get me killed in some Abdijan back alley.

On one of the last days of the trip, we were picking up things downtown. Mama Okoro sent Nkechi to go get something from a store and we stayed in the car. She took that opportunity to make plain what was on her mind. In her distinct high-pitched voice and accent, she let me know that she didn't want Nkechi and me living together before we were married. Form her point of view, Nkechi was still a member of the Okoro family and therefore should not be cohabitating with me. Only after she became a member of the Carroll family via marriage would I have her blessing for us to live together because then she would be part of my family. Somewhere in the lecture she also let me know that she did in fact like me, which was a relief. I was not offered a chance to insert any input. I simply nodded my head and answered, "Yes, ma'am." I don't think I shared the details of that conversation with Nkechi until we were on the plane headed back to the States. Something about the way the conversation took place signaled that Mama Okoro was laying down the rules as a father would normally do with a suitor trying to court his daughter. I also figured that she had already expressed her views to Nkechi, given how often they communicated, so there was no real urgency to let her know I had also gotten the memo.

I left the Ivory Coast no less resolute to marry Nkechi; however, I also had an understanding that the courtship was going to go the way that Mama Okoro had said it needed to, or else there would be problems. The plans for living together that Nkechi and I had discussed were out the window. We were also going to be celibate until we got married after we had sat through a sermon about the ills of premarital sex. I wasn't sure exactly how going against Mama Okoro's wishes would come back to haunt me, but being amongst Nkechi's extended family for that week, I got the feeling that if I did something to hurt Nkechi or anger Mama Okoro, the family could find ways to deal with me, depending on the degree of my transgression. It's a belief I carry with me to this day. Mama Okoro's sisters are all educated moguls who travel the world as they please, so there are resources. Their extended kinship network is filled with powerful people, which makes it easy to see how they could put a plan in motion to make me disappear if necessary. I say all of this tongue in cheek, but the trip made me more appreciative of their closeness. When we returned from the Ivory Coast, I continued to be drawn further into the Okoro family web.

When we first started dating, Mama Okoro spent more than nine months out of the year in the Ivory Coast and later Tunisia. This meant that as far as local parenting, Nkechi leaned on her aunt and uncle for guidance. The Okerekes lived in Voorhees, New Jersey, when I met them in 2000. The house was very large, and what struck me was that there always seemed to be family staying with them. Their house was also the place where the family gathered for holiday occasions like Thanksgiving and Christmas. The Okereke children never seemed to lack for cousins to hang with and keep them company. I thought they were so well mannered for kids whose parents always seemed to be so laid-back. What I quickly came to understand was that the Okerekes were a unifying force in the family because of their welcoming demeanor and centralized location. Uncle Enyi in particular was a father figure to not only Nkechi but a number of her cousins whose fathers were not in the picture. I had a profound respect for him because on top of being a renowned orthopedic surgeon at the Hospital of the University of Pennsylvania (HUP), he somehow managed to balance all of those demands with this huge family life that extended well beyond his own three children. And he did it all seemingly without ever having to raise his voice.

Nkechi told me many stories about how when she was in school, she would often stop by to see the Okerekes on the weekends to hang when she was on her way back to campus from New York. Whenever she talked about them, there was an adoration about how their team operated and how their doors were always open to family. As time went on, I drew a great deal of insight from observing Uncle Enyi as a father and husband. He was attentive to both while he also excelled in his profession, a skill I find critical for a husband to develop. He and Aunty Toks moved in and out of various social circles with ease and displayed the same level of humility whether they were associating with the Association of Nigerian Physicians in the Americas (ANPA) as they were in their Boule chapter. On top of that, he never lost sight of his Nigerian roots and spent time finding ways to increase the quality of health care available in his native village. When Uncle Enyi tragically passed away in 2008 after he suffered a heart attack while he was visiting

Nigeria, it was a crushing blow to the family. It was like a village losing its chief or a small town losing its mayor. He embodied all that I aspire to be as a man in terms of leading a family, pursuing a career, contributing to his community both financially and politically, and mentoring youth. The way that the Okerekes related to each other was a blueprint for how we would later try to behave as husband and wife. Our relationship has been strengthened by the time we spent with them over the years. Meeting the Okerekes in that first summer of dating Nkechi elevated my sense of Nkechi's family as I continued to evaluate her as a franchise player.

Both the NFL and NBA have draft combines where teams have the chance to size up potential franchise players and prospects get a chance to show off their skill sets in the hopes of getting drafted. The initial months of a relationship are just like the combine in that both parties are able to gather a great deal of information about each other that may ultimately lead to the offering of that coveted max contract in a platinum setting. In the first summer that I dated Nkechi, she stuffed the stat sheet with data confirming that she was a "can't miss" draft pick. Mel Kiper Jr., draft expert, would've had her at the top of his big board. Not only did she pass the eyeball test in her measurables like height, weight, eye color, and hair length, but so did her intangible measurements. She believed in family. She had a clear vision of how she wanted her career to play out, and she proved throughout that first summer that she was in my corner, understood the "we are one" philosophy, and would hang with me through trials and tests of our commitment to each other.

In spite of the effort that Nkechi and I were making to see each other as often as we could, burning up the New Jersey Turnpike in the process, there was a lot of time when we weren't together, and as a twenty-five-year-old young professional, there were times that I desired female company in the spaces when Nkechi wasn't in town. Even with the knowledge that Nkechi was a keeper and that I didn't want to lose her, it didn't stop me from making stupid decisions that would put the whole thing in jeopardy. Temptation for quick frolic sessions was all around, as I was still living close to Philly, which meant there were multiple past partners in the vicinity. When you added to that the number of fraternal and citywide social events that were available, the job of staying focused and committed became more difficult. Often in church, Bishop Ulmer, will talk about how the devil knows just the right buttons to push to make you fall. He knows your vulnerabilities and fashions trials just for you. I always nod in agreement because that has certainly been my experience.

In the summer of 2000 I got to do a lot of hanging out when I wasn't coaching. I had my Penn folk who were finishing up their degrees, and I also spent a lot of time on campus advising undergrads in my fraternity. There were also ex-girlfriends like Nina around who had returned home after graduating college. Whenever we were in the same town, we inevitably ended up speaking or seeing each other because we had a number of mutual friends. We got on good enough speaking terms that we ended up going to see the remake of *Shaft* featuring Samuel L. Jackson. In hindsight, this was a mistake because when you share a relationship history with someone, particularly when that relationship included sex, there is always going to be a slippery slope from a casual encounter to frolic session. Given my feelings for Nkechi and the level of commitment I had to her, going to the movies was crossing the line. Among others things, it sent the signal that I was available when I wasn't, and it was wrong. I wanted to believe that I was the dude who could have all kinds of female friends while I still had a girlfriend just because I liked being the good guy who was celebrated by all. The reality is that when you're in a relationship, the dynamics with female acquaintances must change out of respect for your franchise player. It is the only way to make the relationship work over the long haul.

Clearly I wasn't in full grasp of this concept back then because I compounded the first mistake of going to see *Shaft* by going with Nina to see *Nutty Professor II* on the very next night! When I told Nkechi about seeing *Shaft* the night before, she had been lukewarm about it, but by the second night she was clearly not happy with my choices and let me know as much. Dumb ass that I am, I tried to reassure her that there was nothing to be upset about because Nina was just a friend who knew that I had a girlfriend. Again I really wanted to believe this rationale. I wasn't at the level of maturity to understand that you don't always get to have your cake and eat it too. So with that flawed mind-set, of course I didn't see a problem going to a movie at ten o'clock with

Nina and going to her place afterward. Hanging out and having a fuzzy navel or two couldn't hurt either, right? To add insult to stupidity, I got stung by a bee, which had my hand and face swelling, so I ended up sleeping on Nina's couch.

I called Nkechi as soon as I got up and was headed home fully prepared to beg for her forgiveness after she told me it was over. I didn't get her on the phone, but when she did call me later in the day, I threw myself on the mercy of the court. Of course she had been trying to reach me all night, and when she couldn't, she had imagined the worst. Mama Okoro, who was in town staying with Nkechi, had added her two cents by saying something to the effect of, "I told you not to get so excited over a man." Somehow I managed to convince her it would never happen again. As with many lessons in my life, I had to learn the hard way that when you toe the line with arrogance, you are bound to get burned. These days if I even creep up toward the line of disrespect, I think back to that incident. As Nkechi would later confirm, that night was the closest we've ever come to breaking up.

The summer of 2000 was also an Olympic year, and I had the good fortune of working for a prestigious club with a legendary coach named Richard Shoulberg. Coach Shoulberg had coached multiple Olympic athletes in his career and added to that tally in 2000 when Maddy Crippen became an Olympian in the four-hundred-meter individual medley. By virtue of my work with the club, I ended up getting to travel to a bunch of the big meets that summer, including the Olympic Trials itself in Indianapolis. This meant that I was on the road for two weeks straight and was not in town to help Mike move out of our college apartment and into our new bachelor pad.

Unbeknownst to me, Nkechi coordinated with Mike to come down from New York and meet him at the new apartment so she could set up my room. I remember that as I drove the eleven hours from Indy to Philly, I was dreading going through all the boxes and arranging furniture in the new place. When I walked into that apartment after two weeks on the road and found my room all set up, it was a huge relief. The only thing that could have made it better would've been if Nkechi had been there in person to welcome me, but work prevented that. However, the fact that she had done it was not lost on me, and just in case I didn't understand the magnitude of the gesture, Mike made sure to weigh in with how impressed he was. He let it be known early on that he thought Nkechi was a keeper. I assured him that it was duly noted. I just wanted to be in a better financial position before I got down on one knee. I would soon realize that in the big picture, improving my finances should not have been a deterrent to moving forward.

By the fall of 2001 Nkechi and I had been together for more than a year. It seemed like time had flown by. Nkechi and I were still making our turnpike love work. Often I would leave Bensalem on a Friday night after work and stay with Nkechi for the weekend, and she would often come down to Bensalem and stay with me. In adherence to the rules laid down by Mama Okoro, we did not move in together, and we also were abstaining from sex following the Ivory Coast sermon.

I was in my first year as a lead third-grade teacher at Moorestown Friends School (MFS) in the fall of 2001. After two years at Germantown Academy I realized that I wanted to be an elementary teacher, and MFS gave me that opportunity. It was tough to leave Germantown Academy, as I had been embraced by the whole campus.

They gave me my first opportunity to teach and created a position for me in the history department in my second year so that I could stay. The head of school genuinely seemed to care about my development as an educator as did Coach Shoulberg about my coaching career, but I could not pass up the chance to lead my own classroom. My consolation was that I remained on the coaching staff of the swim club and made the forty-five-minute trek from Moorestown to Fort Washington three times a week. I was very happy with the setup because I had the opportunity to advance my career as an educator while I also continued to coach, which had become a passion of mine. Life was all good until the morning of September 11 rocked my whole perspective.

I don't remember anything special about that morning until the moment when the assistant to the head of the lower school came into my classroom. She was clearly distressed, and began to explain to me what had happened. At first I didn't understand the urgent need to speak to me as she was explaining about a plane crash, but when she said the words World Trade Center, my thoughts immediately went to Nkechi, whose office at the Federal Reserve Bank was only blocks away. The assistant generously said she would watch my class while I ran outside to try to call Nkechi. Ironically just as I got outside, Nkechi called me, but my reception was bad, and we got cut off. I tried calling back, but there was nothing but busy signals. The lines would remain tied up for much of the rest of the day. At this point I started screaming at my phone as I stomped around outside of the school meeting house.

MFS is a Quaker school, and the Quaker mode of worship is to sit in silent reflection inside of a meeting house. My ranting was interrupting the upper-school worship session, which had already begun in order to try to make sense of the day's tragedy. A teacher had to come outside to inform me that I could be heard clearly inside the building. I composed myself after this and made my way back to my classroom. At the very least I had the knowledge that Nkechi was still alive, but I couldn't think straight as I dealt with the uncertainty of her safety. I am thankful that I had a classroom full of children to care for that day. Otherwise I might have gone crazy. I effectively went into autopilot mode for the rest of the school day because the next clear memory I have is that shortly after school ended I got a much-needed phone call from Aunty Toks letting me know that she had heard from Nkechi and that she was fine.

Shortly after Flight 11 hit the North Tower of the World Trade Center, she had been ushered into the vault of the Federal Reserve. You may remember it from *Die Hard: With a Vengeance,* as Samuel L. Jackson and Bruce Willis protected it from being robbed of all the gold stored in it. While this may have been a secure area during the uncertain time when we didn't know if another wave of attacks was coming to New York, the concern of the Fed workers was that they would run out of oxygen. When she recounts the details of that day, Nkechi often notes how it seemed like they were in there for days, while in actuality it was close to three hours. When she was released from the vault, the workers spent some time on one of the lower floors of the Fed before they were released. Nkechi and two of her coworkers made the one-mile walk from the Fed over the Brooklyn Bridge and into Brooklyn, where Okey was able to pick her up. Relief is not a strong enough word to explain how I felt when I was finally able to talk to her on the phone.

Selfishly I wished I could have been there to physically hold her and comfort her as she told me stories of what it was like experiencing the tragedy firsthand with her coworkers. I remember the TV footage of people who made their way out of the city, soot-covered and shocked. There were also the stories of family members who had loved ones in the towers who did not know if they would see them again. There were also stories of heroic first responders who rushed into the towers, knowing that they would likely not exit the building. With all of those images in my head, it became clear that the time of Nkechi just being my girlfriend needed to come to an end quickly. I had almost lost her on that day, and watching the anguish rush over families that received news that their loved ones weren't coming home only drove the point home further. It was one of those moments where you realize that life is fleeting and that each day is a gift. The September 11 tragedy put an end to the beliefs I had about needing to be in a certain financial or career position before I could propose that we become husband and wife. My love and support was good enough, and the rest we could figure out together. Had she died on that day, I would've been robbed of the chance to know how a life with her would unfold. What would coming home from work to her be like? What would raising kids with her be like? I already knew that I wanted to have all these experiences with her, so why not make that explicit? Waiting until Christmas as I had originally planned seemed silly after 9/11. So I began to think about an appropriate time to put the max contract on the table.

Nkechi provided me with one last example that she was indeed my franchise player when she traveled with me to Clermont, Florida, to watch me participate in the 2001 Great Floridian Triathlon, an iron-man distance race composed of a 2.4-mile swim, 112-mile bike, and 26.2-mile marathon run. I had taken up competing in triathlons shortly after graduating from college as a way to stay in shape and had quickly become addicted to the sport. I was already a swimmer and had briefly competed in cross-country as a middle school athlete, so I felt comfortable with two out of the three disciplines. Biking for speed took time to develop, but I had gotten better since completing my first triathlon on a mountain bike. Over the course of a year I prepared for this race, as I was eager to see how I would fare at the iron-man distance. I was impressed by and appreciative of Nkechi's company on the trip, as I figured it would likely take me about twelve hours to finish the race. The fact that someone would hang around and spend her day cheering me on meant a lot. It was definitely the kind of "in your corner" moment that my dad always talked about looking for in a potential partner. As the race day unfolded, Nkechi's support never waned.

I came out the water amongst the leaders, and there was Nkechi cheering. I tried to play it cool as I knew I had a long bike ahead of me and an even longer run; however, having my own personal cheerleader certainly lifted my spirits, and I would need it as the day wore on. Once I got onto my bike, I wouldn't see Nkechi again for six hours as I made my way through the hilly 112-mile course. The bike was always the toughest part of a triathlon for me because my swim strength got neutralized quickly. It didn't take long before the parade of strong cyclists started motoring by, each one of them offering a genuine "Looking good," to which I was always tempted to reply with expletives. I had been raised better than that, so I channeled the anger over being passed into my pedals. When I finally exited the bike and headed out onto the run, I again got to see Nkechi, and I did my best to look like the seven hours of competition had had no effect on me. The run course was a five mile out and back plus three loops of a seven-mile trail that wound through a park, so I got to see Nkechi once per lap. I fashioned myself a pretty good runner, and I always looked forward to the run to see how many of the cyclists I could catch. As I completed the out-and-back and the first loop of the park, I was moving pretty comfortably and was thinking that this race wasn't going to end for me like it does for so many of the ironman athletes I watched on TV over the years when they broadcasted the world-famous Ironman Hawaii event. I would soon learn that all ironman triathletes get humbled at some point during the race when finishing goes from certainty to possibility.

The tipping point for me came on the second loop of the run. I started to feel pain in my chest, and each stride seemed to take more and more effort. I had read a bunch about triathlons in the year leading up to the race, and this seemed normal. I just figured I needed to eat some more food and get some more fluids in me. This did nothing, and by the time I saw Nkechi at the end of the second lap, it took everything for me not to just run off the course and quit. I couldn't even play it cool anymore, so the look on my face as I came through the second lap told Nkechi everything that I was feeling. To her credit, she cheered even more than the previous laps, and that was enough of a spirit lift to keep going.

The story of this adventure couldn't end that I had dragged her all the way to Florida and then did not finish the race. I had to keep going. There were periods where I'd walk a mile, run a mile, but I had to finish. When I did finish, a little more than thirteen hours after I had started, Nkechi was there waiting to give me a congratulatory hug in all my sweaty, funky glory. I was unexpectedly emotional and shed a few tears as the race had certainly pushed me to my limits. She held onto me until I got myself together to go to the recovery tents for some much-needed food. If I had had the strength and a ring, I would've proposed right there because on a day when I had pushed myself to the point of exhaustion, she was right there supporting me the whole time, even when I was clearly falling apart, she cheered. It gave me the sense that no matter what challenge I ever faced personally, she would be there for me, cheering, supporting, and fighting if necessary. The beauty of it all was that it seemed so second nature to her. Of course she was going to accompany me to this triathlon. Of course she was going to cheer her guts out, and of course she was going to give me a massage when we got back to the room so that I'd be able to walk in the morning. She could even play nurse if she had to.

Shortly after I crossed the finish line and hugged Nkechi, I felt good enough to walk over to the recovery tent and grab some much-needed food and drink. As I gorged myself, I started to feel light-headed and ended up sitting on one of the tables that they set up for people who need medical attention with one of those aluminum foil-looking blankets wrapped around me. The medical staff went and found Nkechi, who helped me get back to the car and drove me to the hotel where we were staying. As we pulled up to the hotel, my stomach began to take issue with the mixture of pizza, Gatorade, and energy bars I had been ingesting over the last twelve hours and decided it was going to purge whether I was close to a toilet or not. I was left to make like Maya Rudolph in *Bridesmaids* and just let it happen in the corner of the parking lot. To her credit, Nkechi said nothing as I came into the room and went straight for the shower. When I came out, she gave me a much-needed massage that allowed me to sleep like a baby and get ready for the long drive back to Philly. To have been that vulnerable physically and have her not waver in her support was not lost on me and erased any lingering doubts about wanting her to be that person I would share the rest of my life with.

A few weeks after the trip to Florida for the triathlon, Nkechi planned a trip to the Poconos to celebrate me finishing the race. By this time I had been to visit our family jeweler to see about a ring. I knew he would be able to pick out something tasteful within my price range that would show that I had done my diamond homework. I know many ladies like to take their man to the jeweler and *tell* them which ring they want if and when the time comes, and many dudes go along with it because they don't want to mess it up; however, my approach was that the ring was a symbol of the lifetime contract that I was offering, much like a signing bonus, and that it could always be upgraded at various intervals, so the lady would get her chance to express her opinion on the ring down the road if all went well. After I picked out a nice diamond and setting with Mr. Hyman, my assignment was to figure out Nkechi's ring size, so he gave me a bunch of ring sizers. I brought these with me to the Poconos, figuring I'd be able to sneak them on Nkechi at some point while she was sleep. It didn't quite work out that way in the end.

Whenever Nkechi and I would spend the weekend either in Bensalem or New York, much of the time was spent cuddled up next to each other, watching Lifetime movies. Yes, Lifetime network movies, which often centered on embattled women finding ways to either beat, kill, or professionally destroy the men who had done them wrong. The way I saw it, anytime I got to spend with Nkechi was quality time, so if I had to suck up a couple *Lifetime* movies, then so be it. After we watched one of these movies during our Poconos getaway, I got up the nerve to ask Nkechi to be my franchise player for life. There was no special monologue or poem. I just remember us looking at each other affectionately, and then I said something to the effect of, "What do you think about enjoying time like this as my wife?" She smiled, and I waited for the anticipated "Yes!" But instead she playfully said something like, "I don't know. I'll have to think about it," at which point she realized that I was serious.

Granted, had I gone through all the pomp and circumstance of getting on a knee and pulling a ring out of my pocket, then there wouldn't have been any confusion; however, I thought I had seized a nice tender moment to offer the greatest max contract of all, and she was making jokes. In that moment I was salty at myself and a little at her, so I went silent. Having realized that I had genuinely just asked her to marry me, Nkechi quickly asked me to repeat the question now that she knew it was for real, but in my mind the moment had passed, so I refused, saying that she'd have to wait until I asked again. Clearly I needed to make more of a ceremony of the moment. So we just continued to lie around and watch TV until we got hungry.

The beauty of a place like the Poconos is that you're isolated from everyone so there are few disturbances. The curse of a place like the Poconos is that you're isolated from everyone, so there are few fine dining options. This meant that McDonald's and other fast food joints were the options for the weekend. When I set out to grab dinner, I realized that I had another chance to ask Nkechi to marry me and make it a more memorable moment. When I got to the room, I put all the food on a tray along with a bottle of sparkling apple cider that I had picked up from a local supermarket. I put the tray down and then proposed properly on a knee with my ring sizer in hand. This time Nkechi said yes, and she may have even gotten a little choked up. She put the ring sizer on like it was a four-carat rock, and it was another reassurance that she was the franchise player for me. We left the Poconos excited to share the news with our respective families.

Signing a Lifetime Contract

I will be your man, your protector, your best friend

'til my humble life is ended.

Then time begins again.

—Case

The wedding planning went into full effect the minute we left the Poconos. We delivered the news to my mother in person and then went to see Uncle Enyi to make sure we followed in Nigerian tradition of getting approval from the bride-to-be's father figure. I had gotten Okey's approval to ask for his sister's hand before we left for the Poconos. We stopped on the way to Voorhees to pick up a bottle of Christian Brothers as a token dowry, which Uncle Enyi happily accepted. Over the next nine months before we were to be married in August of 2002, we tried to maintain our sanity and enjoy the process while we kept egos in check and the size of the guest count to a manageable number.

One thing that we did in addition to presenting Uncle Enyi with a bottle of Christian Brothers to respect Nigerian customs was to have a traditional "Knocking on the Wood" engagement ceremony at the Kalus house in Long Island. With Nkechi being one of the first among her cousins to get married, the idea was to have the ceremony so that the younger cousins would have a chance to see how it went. In addition, it would give my family a sense of how things would've gone down had we been in the village. One of the most memorable parts of this ceremony included my parents having to bring a number of items to the event off of a list provided by Mama Okoro as Nkechi's dowry. Items included more alcohol and cash, which were presented to Uncle KMK, who served as the head of the family. The other was a test to see how well I knew my wife-to-be by picking her out of a lineup of women who were all covered by sheets. In the Nigerian village this is a difficult task because they find *every* woman who's built like the bride so that your recognition skills are truly tested. It proved a near impossible task for the fiancée of Nkechi's cousin Gigi, who did have her engagement ceremony in the village. Uche was faced with more than twenty women all built like Gigi, and he stood there nearly in tears because he could not tell which woman was his wife just by looking at their silhouettes. Thankfully for him Gigi had just gotten French tips done on her toenails and had flaunted them in front of Uche in the days leading up to the ceremony. When he saw those French tips, he knew it was his bride and didn't have to face the embarrassment of the engagement being rejected because he couldn't identify her.

My scenario was different in that our ceremony was only about going through the motions. Okey told me that Nkechi would be the second girl to come out before the ceremony, but there was this nagging thought in my head. *What if he's playing a cruel joke on me and it's not really her?* So I paid attention Uche-style as the girls came out and looked at their feet because that was the only thing exposed. Afo noticed this and sought to throw me off the scent by applying orange foundation to her feet. When Nkechi did come out second, I just started laughing uncontrollably, which in turn made Nkechi laugh, and the whole thing was kind of spoiled. I realized, however, how difficult it would've been to pick out Nkechi from a lineup of girls specifically selected because they had similar builds. I was thankful not to have had to travel to the village to face that challenge.

The first sign I got that it might get a little difficult keeping things the way we wanted happened when we started to receive xeroxed copies of our invitation back with people who were not on the original guest list, indicating that they were coming. I remember calling Nkechi at work after I had opened the mail and hearing the frustration in her voice rise as she realized what had happened. Turns out Mama Okoro had made copies of the invitation and passed it out amongst her friends in the Ivory Coast like a graduation announcement. Little did she know that since Nkechi was the first of her children to be getting married, many of them jumped at the chance to be in attendance to celebrate with their friend marrying off one of her children. Many Ivorian friends ended up getting added to the guest count, which we had originally set at 150. By the time we had to give an initial number to the wedding hall, the count was up to 185. What always cracked me up was that my guest count of friends and family came out to around 60 and it took me an hour to figure that out while Nkechi's count took up the remaining 125. Even at 185 we had to be strict about who was coming. There were only so many plates we were looking to pay for.

I didn't realize how much of a racket weddings are for a church until it was my turn to walk down the aisle. Once we agreed to get married in Philly, I pushed for the ceremony to be in the church I had grown up in since I was six. I had been in countless Easter, Christmas, and choir programs and I had occasionally delivered the morning announcements as I got older. On top of that, my dad was a deacon, so it meant something to me to have my pastor perform the ceremony. I started to second-guess that when we were presented the church contract for having a wedding there, which stipulated that we had to hire a church-approved wedding planner to be present for all rehearsals at the church. There would also be an assessment if the wedding started late and ran long. Where many churches had a recommended donation for having the ceremony, my church had a standard fee. When we asked about all of the fees, we were told in so many words that since everybody from the cake baker to the florist to the caterer gets paid handsomely for their services, why shouldn't the church? Eye-opening as all of this was, I still wanted to have the ceremony there. I'd known the pastor since I was six. He'd given me a shout-out in front of the whole congregation after I'd graduated college. I respected him as a man of God and figured the three counseling sessions that we were supposed to have with him before the wedding would make up for the other stuff.

Unfortunately we only got one of those counseling sessions. It happened the day before the wedding. The majority of the session consisted of Nkechi and I recounting the story of how we met and fell in love. We told the pastor the strengths and weaknesses we saw in each other, and then he dismissed us. A session that was supposed to last an hour was over after less than thirty minutes. By that point Nkechi and I were done getting mad about minor stuff and just looked forward to the rehearsal dinner that was about to happen and the wedding ceremony, which would take place the next day. Of course the wedding couldn't go off without one more church snafu that would seriously impact the way I viewed organized religion moving forward.

Though Nkechi and I did not get all the premarriage counseling that we thought we were going to get, it is a worthwhile endeavor to pursue prior to exchanging "I dos." At the very least, counseling programs get you to start thinking about some of the answers to questions that you will face down the road in marriage so that you are not caught off guard. At their best they share strategies for navigating the marriage waters and put you in contact with veteran mentors who share their experiences and talk about how they continue to make marriage work thirty, forty, and fifty years down the road. If the program that is offered at your local church is not satisfactory, you can consult a local marriage and family therapist to see if they offer one-on-one or group counseling.

As I stood at the altar on my wedding day with my best man at my back, I couldn't help but smile. The church was decorated. The guests looked great, and I was about to exchange vows with Nkechi that we'd be partners until death did us part. Once she made her way to the altar in her formfitting, strapless dress, I even joked with her about how her shaking flower bouquet showed her nervousness. She laughed, and the service proceeded. It seemed like no time before we got to the "You may kiss the bride" part, and then we were off down the aisle as newlyweds. But then the record skipped. My pastor, the one I'd known for almost twenty years, the one who had baptized me at eighteen, concluded the ceremony by announcing to the guests, "It gives me great pleasure to introduce you to Mr. and Mrs. Jonathan Okoro!" I remember turning to look back as I heard the wrong last name echo through my ears but then just smiled and shook my head. It was a fitting end to what had been an eye-opening experience with my home church. We'd effectively been treated like we had never set foot in that church prior to the wedding. Of course there had to be a moment like that on the day of the actual wedding. I wasn't going to let it spoil the day for Nkechi and me. It was time to celebrate with our family and friends. First we had to take the all-important wedding photos.

It had been an ordeal to select the wedding photographer. The dude we settled on came to us by virtue of Nkechi signing up for a lot of services on a wedding website and earning a coupon for a vacation that we had to go to the photographer's office to redeem. When we got to the Long Island office, we had to hear his sales pitch about the package he could offer us, and he eventually won us over by adding an oil painting of a photo of our choice to the package. We were impressed by the sample that was on his wall and signed on the spot. On the wedding day we found that he was not the only photographer who would be working that day. The whole wedding party was set up to take our first shot when all of a sudden we heard a voice with a distinct African accent calling for us to "look this way." Everyone kept smiling, but Nkechi and I through our teeth were saying "Who is that guy?" As it turned out, one of Nkechi's aunts had hired a photographer from Nigeria to come work the ceremony so that he could send pictures back to go in the local newspaper. When I shook the man's hand, he let me know in no uncertain terms how fortunate I was. "You are a *very* lucky man," he told me. He went on to tell me how blessed I was to be marrying into the Okoro family because they were like royalty in their Nigerian village. He also told me how his photos would be in a big spread in the paper, which they were, but he needed to fall back a smidge, given that he was a subcontractor. Between the photographer we hired taking up most of my reception happy hour and the Nigerian photographer being impatient, the photography at our wedding became a slight nuisance. Thankfully the pictures came out looking good.

When I look at those pictures today, I am reminded of how calm I was throughout the day. I was marrying the woman whom God blessed me to be with, and I was happy to have found her at such a young age. I believe that we are all flawed, incomplete individuals and that marriage is a way of providing that completeness and balance through a covenant with God. The Bible makes it plain in Genesis 2:18: "It is not good for the man to be alone. I will make a helper suitable for him" (MSG). Genesis 2:24 explains further, "That is why a man leaves his father and mother and is united to his wife, and they become one flesh" (MSG). When I watched my parents light the unity candle with Mama Okoro at our wedding as a symbol of the union of our families, I very much felt the spirit of those scriptures, and that was exciting to me. The commitment that marriage requires was not daunting because as far as I was concerned, I was gaining more than I could possibly be losing. Yes, my behavior would have to change in how I related to other women. Yes, I was committing to a life with only one sexual partner moving forward, but I was gaining a cheering squad that would never let me hang my head, a woman I knew would be a great mother and would continually challenge me to be a better man.

Often when I hear other men talking about their hesitance to get married, I don't think they fully grasp the benefits they are gaining versus their perceived losses. In the sports sense they are the owners more worried about the signing bonus they are offering instead of understanding that the bonus will be chump change compared to the money they will make when that player helps them win multiple championships. What was wonderful about Nkechi was that she never put pressure on me to propose. She let her game speak for itself. In fact, because of her approach, her cousins Afo and Ogori felt the need to have us come out for a lunch at Jimmy's Café in the Bronx to try to bully a proposal out of me. As they not-so-discreetly ushered Nkechi to the bathroom so that they could badger me alone, Nkechi initially refused to go because she knew what was going on. She was adamant that she didn't need to go to the bathroom because she was already fine with the state of our marriage discussions. She made it clear through her actions that she could walk away if I wasn't going to recognize and honor her commitment to me. The patience she showed in me then and continues to exhibit even now has been critical to the continued development of our marriage. I asked my panel how they knew that their partners were the ones with whom they wanted to spend the rest of their lives.

Ali: I could see my mother's love in her eyes.

Royale: What I recognized in her was a person that gave me something that was beyond just the lust of sex and, there's a trust there that I could build something with her that was more than just a sexual experience. I trust her to carry everything that I want to put forth in the world in children... She was interesting enough to me to want to continue this journey through the rest of my life.

O'Neil: The connection was there. I felt as though this was someone who in a certain sense brought me out [of] my shell, brought me out of my comfort zone as well. I felt like we were on the same page.

Terrence: I would say on a personal friendship level, the open and candidness that she has. You realize this person trusts in you a lot. They're willing to be emotionally vulnerable to you. Therefore to me I took that to see that that's someone who also knows the importance of emotions and how to be a good shepherd of someone's emotions.

Part 2

The Newlywed Years

The Newlywed Years

Grow old with me! The best is yet to be.

—Robert Browning

Once rookie athletes are drafted by organizations, they go through the process of getting familiar with their new environments. They have to figure out where to live, where to bank, the cool places to hang out around town. They also have to figure out what their organization expects from them and communicate with the organization about any special needs they may have to make them more effective. All of these same adjustments happen with newlywed couples. Living arrangements change, and the couple has to figure out how to blend the stuff they have into one dwelling. They have to figure out how to cohabitate so that they don't get on each other's nerves. We get to see what this is like every football season when HBO's *Hard Knocks* follows a football team from preseason to the first kickoff. Rookies inevitably make all kinds of mistakes as they try to fit within a new organization. In the particular case of the high draft picks who are expected to become franchise players, they have the added weight of expectations to deal with as they try to learn everything there is to know.

Nkechi and I settled nicely into being able to live together. We complemented each other in ways that kept conflict to a minimum. She liked to cook. I didn't mind doing dishes (or feeding them into the dishwasher). Neither of us minded washing clothes or folding them. One rookie mistake that we did make was thinking that we needed to go out and buy a whole lot of grown-up furniture for our first apartment as if it was our Ken and Barbie dream house that we were going to live in for the next twenty years. The salesperson at Raymour & Flanigan must've seen that newlywed glint in our eyes when we walked into the store, looking for dining room, living room, and bedroom sets. We also fell for the 0 percent financing for a year, as we thought there was no way we wouldn't pay off our $5,000 in furniture purchases within twelve months. Not a smart investment in the long run because as I look around the house today, there are only three pieces in the house that are still being used. Less than half the stuff we bought on that day made the trip to California when we moved.

The reason why this mistake is one that Nkechi and I can joke about today is that we were both on the train of thought that said, "You're married now! Gotta furnish your crib like grown folk do." It's critical in the early part of your marriage to learn how to move as one so that you establish a routine of communication on decisions that should be made jointly and you can own a decision as a couple so that it doesn't become a thing where one person is sitting there with the screwface and thinking, *I told you we should've done what* I *said*. Our first year of marriage was like an extended honeymoon because we rarely disagreed, and when it came to the house, we both did our part to keep it looking right.

This may seem trivial, but given Nkechi's profession, it would've been selfish to expect that she should come home from work, cook, wash clothes, and be the only one maintaining the house. A husband is silly to think that his franchise player wife can work a full day, maintain a house by herself (which gets harder with kids), and not develop some kind of animosity toward him at some point.

A husband has got to find a way to support the house beyond providing monetary resources. A division of labor is critical to keeping a household going, and it's ideal to keep that division fluid. I have to laugh when I hear men and women talk about man jobs versus women jobs. When you are trying to keep a marriage together and particularly when children are introduced into the equation, they are just jobs that need to get done, and it is up to husband and wife to communicate about how those jobs get done based on schedules, skills, etc. The same approach should be true when managing household economics.

I'm an educator by training and by passion, which means that I have always made less than Nkechi. Over the years that gap has closed as I accumulated more degrees and ascended the coaching ladder. We have always managed to maintain a healthy dynamic about finances because neither of us have ever been selfish with the resources that we've amassed. Nkechi has understood my student loan debt and less than stellar credit rating, and I've tried to honor that by working my ass off to make sure she never perceives me as a financial deadweight. It's not like her Penn degree was free. She had financial obligations of her own coming into our relationship. No matter what each of us is making, our household stands on a foundation of communication and consensus. Having the bigger checking account balance does not carry more cache when it comes to making major decisions. I'm also in no way emasculated by the fact that Nkechi grosses more than I do. I have a career. I contribute to the household according to our game plan, and I do whatever else I need to do to make sure Team Carroll stays on course. I do understand how easy it is for men who fall on hard times to start doubting themselves when their wives become the only breadwinners. Mike is in a similar position at home and described his outlook this way:

> You could say we're nontraditional in that she's the primary breadwinner, but you know to me, I do well enough to take care of me you know what I mean? I don't rely on her to pay my bills or ask her to do this, that and the other you know what I mean? I would be just fine on my own doing what I do now.

There's more on this topic to come, but what was important at the newlywed stage was that our finances never stopped Nkechi and me from enjoying each other's company whether we spent a lot or a little. The majority of my gentlemen panel expressed a similar outlook to mine in terms of household labor division.

O'Neil—At this point it's just a job that needs to get done really. I mean we kinda have like general things that maybe [each of us] do. She makes my vegetables for the morning and she's home more than I am during the week at least before me so she'll cook but I'll do the dishes and clean up... It's not divided up by gender lines at all, it's more so just when things need to get done.

Ali—You know we just do the duties as time permits. When I'm not at work, I watch the kids. I do homework every day with my daughter. I love this.

Mike—It's not etched in stone she does this I do that. I don't think it can be that. You gotta be flexible, you know, we both may be better at certain things than the other person. With her job, her schedule and travel, sometimes I gotta be able to fill that void and then the same thing for her you know if I'm on the road.

Friday night or Saturday night was date night for Nkechi and me throughout the years before we had little ones. It was our way to slow down the carousel we're on during the week and just have some time to be with each other and check in. Often it was as simple as hitting the local Applebee's and then seeing whatever movie was opening that weekend. Before movie ticket prices became equal to buying tickets to a concert, a Friday night date would cost us less than thirty bucks. (Gotta love the student discount at the movies.) Date night also meant a lot of driving up the Jersey Turnpike to hang with Nkechi's family, her coworkers, or Penn folk. The drive to and fro was time to catch up, make plans, listen to music, gossip, and develop our dynamic to the point where we could finish each other's sentences. Or we didn't have to talk at all. We were that comfortable until I made a lane change she didn't like, and then I'd have to hear about it. Our newlywed years were also when we started our tradition of going to concerts.

For a concert date to work, both parties have to enjoy the artist at least a little, or one party is just sitting there salty for three to four hours while the other sings along to every song. Fortunately my music taste spans enough genres that when Nkechi and I go to a concert, both of us enjoy not only being with each other but watching the performance itself. Then there is something to discuss afterward. For our first anniversary, we went to see Justin Timberlake and Christina Aguilera as they co-headlined the Stripped Tour. They also had this up-and-coming group named The Black Eyed Peas opening for them. They have turned out to be a pretty big deal. What was notable about the concerts we took in back then was that they created a catalog of shared experiences that we could look back on and laugh about, whether they were highlights or lowlights in particular cases.

In April of 2003 my mother bought Nkechi and me tickets to see Anita Baker in Atlantic City. This was notable for two reasons. The first was that my mother had raised me on Anita Baker. Prior to finding hip-hop, Anita Baker stood out for me among a number of great soul artists. Secondly Anita Baker had hardly been touring since the release of her *Rhythm of Love* album in 1994, so to catch her performing live was a treat. The date of the concert just happened to coincide with a field trip Nkechi's acting class was taking to see a play being put on in Connecticut. When she told me, everything about my body language must've said, "You've got to be kidding me," because she quickly assured me that we would make it from Connecticut to South Jersey in time for the concert. Only when you love someone are you willing to go along with stuff you *know* makes absolutely no sense, but there I was riding up to Connecticut on the same day as the Anita Baker concert. It didn't take long to realize the day wasn't going to go as planned.

Not only were we driving from Plainsboro, New Jersey, to Hartford, Connecticut, a three-hour ride, but we were making stops in New York to pick up some of Nkechi's classmates. At this point I went into silent mode, my retreat when I am feeling a certain way about the situation at hand but I don't want to blow up. It's like when Martin Lawrence had to rub his ears and chant *Wooosah* in *Bad Boys 2*. I have no memory of anything about the play because I was getting madder with each minute that I was sitting there. When we left the theater, it was already five o'clock, and we not only had to take home the classmates that we brought, but we somehow managed to pick up another classmate. At this point I started having the most profane conversation in my head that I could imagine. *What the f@#! is going on here? In what alternate world are we gonna get from Connecticut to Atlantic City in three hours? With three stops! This is some bullshit!*

By the time we dropped everyone off and made it back to the Plainsboro area, it was already past 8:00 p.m., and I was having a different conversation in my head because now it was real that I was going to miss part of the show. I started calculating scenarios. *If we get there by 9:30 p.m., then maybe we'll catch her as the opening act is getting off stage. If the show doesn't start till 8:45 p.m., then maybe we'll get to see her whole set. What concert ever starts on time? F*#@! I can't believe I'm going to miss this show.*

Nkechi said nothing the whole time we were driving and just focused on driving her Nissan Maxima like it was a low-flying jet. We averaged more than ninety miles per hour as we rolled the distance from Plainsboro to Atlantic City, and I couldn't believe that we didn't see one cop the whole way. Clearly God had mercy on us this day and blessed us with traveling grace because there's no way I would've been able to make that drive at that speed in that car and *not* see an officer of the law. We made it to Atlantic City in what had to be some kind of record.

When we walked into the theater, Anita Baker was already on stage and well into her set. The final dagger in my heart was that the seats were great. Dead center on the floor maybe twenty rows in. I got to enjoy four songs, and that was it. The concert was over. I don't even think Ms. Baker did an encore that night. By this time Nkechi was mortified, and she tried her best to make it right by offering to get us a room at the casino so that it was not a total loss; however, I wanted no parts of it. I just wanted to go home, and that's what we did. I drove home, and of course now that I was behind the wheel, the cops were out in full force, so I couldn't really take my aggressions out on the road like I wanted. Again traveling grace was on our side because on any other occasion I would've gotten a ticket (or two) for sure. Thankfully a $300 speeding ticket is not an additional footnote to my sad Anita Baker story.

Concerts are a special kind of date night because often we get dressed up for them and really make it an event. They are like successful road trips for a team. When teams have success on the road, their bonds become stronger, and they become a better unit. The same is true when couples take the time on a regular basis to have special moments with each other away from friends and family. Each event is like a brick being laid on a strong foundation. The more fortified the foundation, the better the structure will be able to withstand tumultuous events like storms and earthquakes. Nkechi and I are certainly better off as a couple because of those early years when it was just the two of us. We really got the chance to establish an identity as a couple and get a sense of the direction that we wanted to travel in together on the fruits of our individual labor.

As our first anniversary neared in the spring of 2003, we were both looking at major changes in our careers. Though Nkechi had risen to the point at the Federal Reserve where she was participating on weekly phone calls with the Federal Reserve chairman, Allen Greenspan, she was ready to take her pursuit of life as an actress to the next level, and that meant moving to California. Ever since I had first heard Nkechi talk about eventually leaving the Fed to act, I knew the day would come when she would say, "It's time to go," and I did not blink when she did. I had observed over the years that when Nkechi sets her mind to a task, she was methodically relentless in pursuing it. I never had any real worry about it not working out because of her drive. As far as my career, I felt that with the two years that I had put in at Moorestown Friends plus the master's degree that I was finishing, it wouldn't be hard to find a teaching job in California or a coaching position. I figured that I had built up enough professional cache that I wouldn't be out of work for long once we got there. Our first year of marriage had flown by, and it seemed easy, so uprooting and leaving our families and friends really didn't seem that daunting.

The impending move was also made less intimidating by the fact that it wasn't necessarily going to be permanent. Nkechi and I agreed that we would revisit staying on the West Coast in five years. If we were struggling and wanted to come home, we could. When we talk with people about our move, many are surprised that I was willing to drop everything and move, but for me it was a welcome opportunity to be somewhere other than the East Coast. I had grown up in Philly, gone to college fifteen minutes from home, and was now living only an hour away, so the chance to experience a new environment with my franchise player was a win-win situation for me. When we went to California to do some preliminary scouting in March of 2003, I was instantly comfortable with Los Angeles and its surrounding areas. We reconnected with Lauren Thibodeaux, a friend from college, which made the process of getting acclimated in Southern California much easier. I had met Lauren through Terrance and had stayed in contact with her through the years. She was a California native, and when she took us to dinner, we got a good sense of all that SoCal life entails—great scenery, monster traffic. Lauren's family also treated us like we were Thibodeaux. It gave me the sense that we could rebuild the type of social network that we had on the East Coast, which was one of my biggest concerns.

Of additional concern for me was not adding to the pressure that Nkechi was feeling to make good on her intended career change. Not only did she want to prove to herself that she could do it, but there was also a feeling of *I'm taking Jon away from his family*, a valid concern when you consider how protective both my mother and Nana had been over the years. There was also the notion that in Nigerian families, you don't pursue the arts. Where is the money in that? Nkechi had gone into banking not only because she could keep her numbers straight but also because it was a career choice that was approved by Mama Okoro. Among Nkechi's family and many like hers, the acceptable careers are medicine, law, and business. Her announcement that she was going to pursue a career in entertainment was met with skepticism. Being on the wrong side of the Okoro clan is not a kind place to be, so I tried to make sure that I was as supportive as possible. As it turned out, we would need to support each other a lot as we made the transition.

We landed at LAX to stay on January 1, 2004. We spent the night in a hotel in Culver City because we weren't going to be able to move into our apartment in Sherman Oaks until the next day. Even when we were able to move in, we could only do so much because our furniture was not arriving for another couple of days. Once we checked out of the hotel, we set about learning the area around our apartment and started to take care of logistical things like going to the DMV, locating the closest supermarket, and beginning to find jobs. All of these seemingly minor chores proved to be more difficult and time-consuming than we had originally thought they would be. If we had not had eighteen months already invested into our marriage, then things might have gone differently. The early days of our California adventure were definitely a test of how tight we really were.

We got a clear wake-up call that California living wasn't going to be all sun and fun on our first night living in our apartment. As expected, the Mayflower truck carrying our stuff from the East Coast had not yet arrived; however, we had packed blankets and pillows, and we figured that sleeping on the floor one night wouldn't be that big a deal. After all, we were living in the San Fernando Valley, which is known to be five to ten degrees hotter than oceanfront cities like Santa Monica on any given day. So as we lay down on our makeshift bed, we quickly realized that this thought process was all wrong, and we damn near froze to death that night in our empty apartment. The first thing we did the next day was go to the Linens 'n Things and get a comforter because a second night sleeping at that temperature wasn't going to happen. We were similarly naïve in our approach to finding jobs to support us while we were living the "starving artist" life.

Neither of us thought that we'd ever be in a position where we couldn't find work. Between the Ivy League and master's degrees, we thought that finding jobs would not be that difficult, particularly work that would allow Nkechi to pursue auditions. It was like the player who feels that his resume is good enough that he should still be playing in the league but for whatever reason can't get a tryout. For Nkechi, it became laughable when she couldn't get a job as a hostess at a restaurant. My low point came when I was all set to accept a position selling sneakers, but I ultimately didn't get it after they ran a credit check on me. I also wasn't having any luck finding work as a coach initially, so it really began to look like we might be one of those couples who head out west looking to set the world on fire only to return six months later with our tail between legs. Our families really stepped up during this time, helping us with funds to keep us afloat, and we continued to pound the pavement and make the sacrifices necessary to get by.

One of those early sacrifices was trading in Nkechi's Nissan Maxima, which she had bought in 2003 shortly after my car died. She gave me her old Maxima and treated herself to the sleeker, more powerful version. That car served us well in the time that we had it, and we were both sad to see it go; however, the size of the monthly payment didn't fit with our new household budget. In place of the Maxima, we got a 2002 Nissan Altima, which became the workhorse of the family as we could only afford one car at the time. This made it very interesting logistically when Nkechi and I finally did manage to get regular jobs.

After two months of trying to find a gig that would allow Nkechi to pursue auditions and classes, she came to the realization that it was better to have a job in her field that would allow her to pay the bills than have no job and plenty of time to be an actress. She found a gig at the LA office of the San Francisco Federal Reserve Bank working in banking supervision and regulation. It worked out well for her because the pace of the San Francisco Fed was slower than what she had been used to in New York. She could therefore finish her assignments quickly and then spend time searching out auditions and preparing for classes. It was this double-duty work ethic that would serve her well as she started to work her way from the outskirts of the Hollywood circle toward the core much like a football player goes from the practice squad to the pro bowl.

For my first couple of months as a Californian, hourly work was all that I could get. I got a job coaching a club swim team after I ran into a college teammate of mine who was on the staff. They needed someone to help the youngest munchkins, so I signed on to work there three days a week. The other days I spent as a tutor at a local Sylvan Learning Center. At the same time I started looking for teaching positions for the next school year and ultimately got one teaching second grade. It was a huge relief to get the job hurdle out of the way because it gave us the reassurance that Nkechi wouldn't be shouldering the bulk of the financial burden much longer and that we could start to plan for our future. Securing a job also helped ease some of the growing tension that our finances were no longer what they had been on the East Coast.

When finances in a marriage get off track or are suddenly lacking, the dynamic between partners will inevitably suffer. What franchise player would want to play for an organization that can't make payroll? In our situation, the fact that I couldn't bring what I brought to the table previously made me feel like I wasn't upholding my end of the bargain. The frustration from being rejected at places like Staples, Sav-On pharmacy, and Ralphs supermarket also started to creep into my decision-making process. Instead of taking the stance that I would do whatever was necessary to make ends meet, I started to be a little selfish and put my priorities ahead of the marriage, figuring that I wouldn't be able to do anything until the teacher-hiring season really got going. Instead of continuing to look for an additional job that might have me working overnight or early in the morning, I chose not to, as those were my designated workout times. This wasn't a popular decision with Nkechi, but thankfully she never flipped out on me about it. She figured that she had moved us in the middle of the school year, so there was a certain amount of rope that she had to give me. Instead of continually harping on it, she decided to leave it alone.

If I had the chance to rewind the tape and do that time over, I certainly would have approached the job hunt differently. Securing a better job earlier on would have allowed Nkechi to focus on planning her Hollywood takeover sooner instead of having to spend so much brainpower on making sure our finances were in order. It also would have shown her that as her partner I was willing to take on whatever role I needed to for the good of the team. Disparity in income between marriage partners is one thing, but when the partner who is making less starts acting like they don't have a role to play in the organization, that's when you have to start questioning the partnership. Thankfully we did find stable financial footing, and we also started to develop a network of friends who helped keep us sane as we adjusted to our new situation. Given what we went through, I was interested to hear what it was like for members of my panel in their early years.

Trent—I think one of the things we started to do was travel. You know, getting away. Taking the time to get away from work and everything else.

Royale—Being in the entertainment business, I'm constantly, at least back then, I was constantly trying to stay on the road, trying to build business opportunities. As a standup comic it would take me out on the road for weekends and days at a time and I just think it adds challenges when you spend so much time away from home.

The process of building our friend network in California started with Nkechi attending an actor's intensive workshop in the spring of 2003 before we moved. She met actors who were already living in SoCal, and her relationships with them ultimately lead to us living in Sherman Oaks. When we hit the ground in SoCal, we started to meet people who were connected to our East Coast friends. Someone would say, "Oh, my homey that I went to college with lives out there. You should look her up." And we would follow through. In addition, we had UPenn alums we knew. We got to the point where we felt good enough about our friends to host our first event in our new abode.

Game nights became a tradition for Nkechi and I before we were married when we'd burn up I-95 to visit our friends and play games like Taboo and Cranium. The games would get heated and competitive because we would only play guys versus girls. The discussions that followed were just as loud and spirited. When we got married, we continued the tradition, and it became a great way for us to get to know other couples or work colleagues as well as catch up with old friends. Our first game night in California was in our little one-bedroom apartment, which was less than eight hundred square feet. We hadn't fully furnished our place yet, so there was a box that we hadn't unpacked with a kente cloth over it that served as our coffee table. Other boxes we hadn't unpacked also got the kente treatment. We didn't have many chairs then, so many people had to sit on the floor. About fifteen folks came over and packed the apartment. We ended up having to keep the doors open because it got so hot. Nevertheless, we had good food and played a great game of Taboo.

Game nights have been a notable part of our marriage not just because of the friends we have made but because they have also given us a way to be social on our own terms. There is a popular notion about Hollywood that people in the business are fake. Folks will gladly smile in your face and act like your best friend out in public only to slice and dice your character behind closed doors. Rarely do people disrespect each other in public because you never know who you might need a favor or job from in the future. We didn't want to have to deal with those types of folks unless absolutely necessary so having the power to choose who came into our home made that less of an issue. Game nights also made it, so we didn't have to feel like we had to play the club scene game in order to be out socially. We've never gone out to a spot where we had to wait in line, hoping to get in, and that won't change. The knowledge that we have a solid network of friends we can go get a drink with and have grown-up conversation with makes the need to be out in a crowded club less desirable. Nkechi downplays any huge role of game nights in our marriage but does acknowledge that the fact that we both enjoy hosting them shows how well we're matched. She notes how hard it would be for us to stay together if I was looking to hit a club every weekend while she would rather curl up on the couch and watch a movie with a glass of wine. Another point of growth for us as we settled into our new California environment was finding a new church home.

The first step we took in finding a church home was to ask our friends where they went. We were aware of the bigger churches in town but were primarily interested in one that would teach us about the Word of God as well as nourish our spirits. For me it was important to find a place of worship that had a lot of Black faces because I wanted to feel connected to a community of parishioners who were facing many of the same issues on a day-to-day basis as I was. Living in the San Fernando Valley does not often afford such an opportunity. Looking forward, I also wanted our place of worship to be a place where our children would be able to grow up as I did in the church and be able to experience the richness and diversity of going to a church where many of the people looked like them. This process took us a while, but ultimately we found a number of places where we were comfortable worshiping on Sundays.

The first church we visited is very well-known and features a distinguished pastor, a choir, and a number of public figures in the congregation. On the Sunday that we visited, the pastor took special time out to recognize one of these members for his work on a recent movie. This wasn't an issue, but opening up the program and seeing the report of who had given what in tithes and offerings the prior week was off-putting. The intrusion of church economics into my Sunday worship diminishes the service and brings into the light a relationship between tither, God, and church that should remain personal. Nevertheless, we waited with anticipation for the sermon. The bishop was as good as advertised as he delivered his message for the day. Nkechi and I were intrigued enough that when the altar call came, soliciting new members, we rose and went to the front of the church to get more information. Unfortunately the induction process for new members was not what we thought it would be.

When we got into the holding room, where they brought all of the people who had come to the pulpit during the altar call, we were immediately given membership paperwork to fill out. I remember thinking that the packet was a bit much, considering that we hadn't indicated the desire to join the church yet. Nkechi had a similar feeling as we both looked at each other and asked one of the church members for clarification. The church worker confirmed that we were indeed filling out membership paperwork, at which time Nkechi and I thanked them for their time and informed them that we were not ready to commit at that moment. It all seemed very pushy to us like they were trying to make some member quota for the month. Needless to say that wasn't the place we joined.

The next church that we visited didn't seem like it would be a good fit just because of the building that service was held in. Even before we moved to California,

I had heard about the church that had purchased the Great Western Forum. As a youth, I watched the Los Angeles Lakers win multiple championships in that building, led by Magic Johnson and Kareem Abdul-Jabbar. Now we were pulling into the parking lot for ten-o'clock service. Our friends had spoken highly of the church in spite of the size, so we figured we could give it an honest try. The reputations of the praise and worship team, congregation, and pastor were all as distinguished as the first church we had visited, so Nkechi and I listened intently to see how the bishop would handle the offering and tithing period. The program we received at the door betrayed nothing about who had and had not given the week prior, so that was a plus. In his remarks the bishop grounded his beliefs about tithing in scripture and talked about the personal obligation of giving as a way to celebrate one's relationship with God. This worked for Nkechi and me, and while we did not get up and go toward the pulpit during the altar call on that first visit, it did make us comfortable enough with the church to come back again. After our fourth visit to Faithful Central Bible Church (FCBC), we did answer the altar call to become members. So began our renewed relationship with organized religion.

While Faithful Central is very much a fit with all of the things that I was looking for in a church, from the dynamic teaching of Dr. Kenneth C. Ulmer to the Sunday school. It is different from what Nkechi grew up with in Nigeria, Cote d'Ivoire, and London. The soulful praise and worship of FCBC is in line with the gospel music I grew up listening to and never fails to lift my spirit. Nkechi grew up with a different style of praise and worship, and it was not until we visited Bel Air Presbyterian one Sunday that I realized the difference. Praise and worship at Bel Air Presbyterian has the feel of a coffeehouse or an indie rock concert, which was more of a fit with Nkechi's music tastes. In addition to the different feel of the music, the senior pastor had a different approach to delivering a sermon than Bishop Ulmer.

It has never been an issue for Nkechi and me to split time at these churches because we like both congregations, pastors, and the programs they offer. We were pleasantly surprised one Sunday to walk into Bel Air and find Bishop Ulmer scheduled to deliver the sermon for one of the joint services that Bel Air does with FCBC at least twice a year. Bishop Ulmer and Dr. Brewer are friends and shared a vision for moving Christianity forward in Los Angeles. Bringing the congregations together periodically was a way to fulfill that vision. Spending time at both churches also provided a variety in experiencing the Word of God.

My personal journey in faith has become increasingly important with each passing year of our marriage because I feel like the strength and discipline necessary to maintain a marriage comes from aligning my life with what God intended marriage to be. It is his covenant that he makes with man and the woman he blesses that man with. As my family has grown, it is my responsibility in raising the kids to have them understand how they are expected to carry themselves. Therefore, I have to be even more attuned with what God's instructions are. Both Ali and Royale had particularly poignant things to say about religion in the household.

Ali—Here's how I feel about teaching kids about spiritual faith. The tenets that many other religions, 'cause I was raised multifaith, teach are basic. And they're great.

Don't hurt people. That's of God. Don't steal. That's of God. Share. Love, give compassion. These are the tenets, these are the principles. There's a lot more like that that are the essence of God. I've found that in between all of them, they preach to be loving. So I'ma do that. Be honest, do that. Do your best do that. Be kind when you can all the time, do that. For these are the unifying principles I find in every faith.

Royale—There is a very clear and understood spiritual base that runs through our household and our relationship and our marriage. There, even outside of me being in this entertainment business um there is a lot of dark forces and energy that pull you away from anything you're trying to do that's positive. So whether it's women whether it's alcohol or if there's business bad intentions, you know there is always things that will pull you away. You remain hopeful, at least I do that your spiritual base, and your connection that you have to your wife um that energy will always be greater than the sum of all the negative forces out there that can pull you away from and distract you from your marriage.

For me there is no more effective way to prop myself up when I am feeling challenged or when temptation comes my way in its many forms. You can talk to friends or your parents, but every marriage is different, so they may not totally understand the problem or offer effective advice. There are also times when I just don't feel vulnerable enough to lay an issue on my partner. The Word and prayer then becomes a powerful tool to help me understand how God has helped others through their struggles and then also allows me to unburden myself. Faith then takes over to bring me through the storm. Given my spiritual growth, I am glad to have a partner who shares the same faith and believes in a similar process. The Bible talks about couples being "equally yoked" or sharing the same faith in 2 Corinthians 6:14–18. The passage essentially asks, "What sense does it make for complete religious opposites to wed because one will inevitably pollute the other?" Given that our spiritual beliefs and religious practices have a great influence on other important family decisions, I cannot imagine what it would be like to have to make those decisions with someone who didn't share the same core religious values. In our early years in LA, having a church foundation really helped buoy us and kept us close as we each tried to find our footing professionally and prepared to start a family.

Additions to the Team

From the first time the doctor placed you in my arms,
I knew I'd meet death before I'd let you meet harm.

—Will Smith

We did as much as we could to plan for when a child would enter our world. We both felt that we wanted to have time to enjoy each other as a couple before we expanded the family, and we also wanted to feel like we were in a position to support a child and be the parents we expected ourselves to be. All that said, we knew that a child would be a blessing from God and that we could really only control when we stopped using contraception. We made this decision early in 2005, believing that we were stable enough in Los Angeles to support a little one and that three years had been enough torture for our families. When we got married in 2002, it was on the heels of two of Nkechi's cousins doing the same. By the time we got to our first anniversary, both cousins had given birth to beautiful children, and Nkechi's family started looking at me as if I had some sort of virility problem. Some even inquired if I needed help. The old African proverb is that it takes a village to raise a child, but the piece they don't tell you is that the man is supposed to be fruitful and help multiply the population of the village. My mother and father said little, but I could tell that Nana wanted a great-grandchild to play with. We stood our ground, however, often pointing out that Nkechi was the first of her siblings to get married and that she was the youngest. How about pressuring some of the other siblings to get married before asking for grandkids? Moving to California was helpful in terms of reducing some of that noise because we didn't get to see our families as often.

We went to the Dallas area to visit Mike and his bride, Kelci, in their Flower Mound, TX home, and it was during this trip that we suspected that the stork had come to visit us. We went out for a great meal on a Friday night and then slept until deep into the afternoon the next day. For me this was no reason for alarm, as I can easily sleep past noon when left to my own devices, but Nkechi is usually an earlier riser. When we did get up, we went out to a local amusement park, and Nkechi was a step slow. She later complained of feeling sick. When we got back to Mike's house that evening, she barely moved off the couch. We agreed that she needed to take a pregnancy test when we got back to California, and I'll never forget receiving the call while on my way to practice and being greeted by the question, "Are you ready to be a daddy?" I was, and when we found out a couple months later that there would be another Carroll man in the family, I couldn't suppress the Kool-Aid smile as I high-fived and hugged my dad, who happened to be in town visiting. In those early months of Nkechi's pregnancy when there was no baby bump, it all just seemed like a wonderful idea. The prospect of a little one in the house was exciting.

The news of Isaiah's coming came around the same time that I had been accepted into the University of California at Los Angeles's (UCLA) doctoral program in education, where I would focus on urban schooling. This meant I would be leaving the classroom, but I had become the second man on the totem pole at Team Santa Monica and was making an okay salary, so I knew I would still be able to help support the baby. I also saw going back to school as a step toward creating the kind of flexible lifestyle that would allow me to be present as a father for my child, which was very important to me. My father had always worked multiple jobs at a time in order to make sure that my siblings and I were cared for, but the cost was that we didn't get to interact with him as much on a day-to-day basis when we were younger. I always felt that his sacrifices were made so that I would have the opportunity to be more physically present for my own children. While I was excited that I would be able to help Nkechi in the all-important early months of Isaiah's life, I was also nervous that somehow I would fall short of being the father I had envisioned. I imagine it is the same feeling as a baseball player who wants to hit a homerun so badly that he swings way harder than he needs to and ends up hitting a foul. It was also a weird time because Nkechi was starting to generate some momentum in entertainment industry circles.

Nkechi's job at the Fed gave her the ability to strategically plan her transition into an entertainment career while she did not have to spend so much time stressing and worrying about how to make ends meet. A large hurdle that most actors face is that the opportunities to showcase themselves are scarce, so many often end up in a money-draining cycle of submitting headshots, going on auditions, taking classes and workshops, but not actually getting to do projects. Nkechi worked this method well enough in our first year in California that she earned her first speaking role on *General Hospital*, the legendary soap opera which happened to be her favorite. With quality technology becoming more affordable and exposure venues like YouTube becoming so viable, Nkechi decided to take more ownership over her career arc and create opportunities for herself to perform. One of the first projects to arise from her new mind-set was to help produce a showcase of one-act scenes in the spring of 2005 that featured an all-woman cast. By that fall she had expanded the scene she performed into a short film titled *Bathroom Break*. The ten-minute project was selected to air at two film festivals and gave Nkechi valuable experience in seeing a whole project through from writing a script to finding a location, securing a crew and equipment, and staying on a budget. Not only did film festival exposure allow her to be seen practicing her craft by those who might later want to hire her, but it also gave her credibility as a multidimensional artist capable of not just interpreting and acting out material but also creating it. That same fall she directed a staging of the play *Autonomy* starring two of our good friends.

I knew she was onto something when she started to do this because with all of the hats that she wore, it allowed her to maximize all of her gifts. I liken it to LeBron James. If he wanted to, he could be the top scorer in the NBA. Scoring, however, is only a part of his skill set. There are probably opposing coaches who try to devise ways to make him only a scorer because then he is not using the other tools in his arsenal to beat them. When he is allowed to handle the ball, rebound, defend, and use his court vision to set up others, he then becomes the multidimensional force that has lead the Miami Heat to back-to-back championships. When Nkechi figured out how to harness her passion for entertainment by putting her imprint all over a production, then she started to make real inroads in Hollywood.

After *Bathroom Break* Nkechi did another short film titled *Apartment A*, which chronicled the aftermath of 9/11 and how three sisters were coping with loss. This project was selected to appear in five film festivals between 2008 and 2009 and enabled Nkechi to keep meeting influential people who wanted to work with her as she gained credibility as a skilled entertainer. She acted in and produced another showcase of one-act scenes in 2008 before she turned her attention to developing a feature-length urban adaptation of *Romeo and Juliet* called *Soar.* This was an all-consuming undertaking, as she not only wrote the script but also outlined the business plan she would use to secure funding. She went out and used her connections to attach talent that she hoped would help attract more money. She did all of this while she was writing spec scripts to apply for network-sponsored writer's programs, working at the Fed, and raising a two year-old child. All I could do was watch in awe and try to keep up.

By the time Isaiah Obiesie Carroll was born on Thanksgiving Day of 2006, I had become the interim head coach of Team Santa Monica. I was given the keys to the organization while the board conducted a national search for a head coach. I had also just finished my first quarter at UCLA, where I was being overwhelmed by the amount of reading required by my program. Between early morning practices, classes, evening practices, and late-night reading, I was in a constant zombie state. I wanted the head coach job, and I was trying to show the board that I was capable of not only keeping the team afloat but also building up our membership numbers. At the same time I was trying to keep up with my classmates at school in the unofficial race to see who would defend their dissertations first. I was also trying to pitch in at home. I was useless when it came to feeding, but I changed diapers and tried to rock the baby to sleep whenever I could. By the end of the winter quarter, things started to get a little easier to handle.

I was named the permanent head coach of Team Santa Monica on April 5, 2007. I will never forget silently fist-pumping like Tiger Woods at Augusta as the board chairperson delivered the news over the phone. I didn't want to wake the baby, so I couldn't let out the primal scream of relief and joy that I would've liked. The team had enjoyed success during the winter season, and the membership numbers had gone up. I was confident that with the interim tag removed, I could continue to help expand the organization, and that's exactly what happened. That summer the team had three swimmers qualify to attend junior nationals in Indianapolis, and the momentum kept building from there. By the summer of 2008 I had completed my doctoral coursework, and the team had its first Olympic trials qualifier. When we arrived at the Qwest Center in Omaha, Nebraska (subsequently named the Century Link Center), where the meet was to be held, I understood what a college basketball coach must feel like when he reaches the Final Four or a baseball manager whose team makes the World Series. In swimming, qualifying athletes for Olympic trials brings instant credibility, and being there that week amongst the biggest names in the sport made all the early practices and sleep deprivation worthwhile. It also meant that I needed to be paid like others who were training that caliber of swimmer and had a similar size program as we had become. Unfortunately the board of directors didn't quite see it that way.

Working with the board of directors of a nonprofit organization is a tenuous deal. You understand that when you sign the contract, if you even get one. Similar to the way hiring a new athletic director at a college can mean a floundering college football coach becomes *Dead*

Man Walking, the turnover of a youth team's nonprofit board can have a similar effect on a coach's job security. The key is to try to craft relationships with parents and influence who is on the board so that you always have a pretty good idea of how many votes you have going in your favor if one or two board members want you out. The 2008 Summer Olympics in Beijing featured Michael Phelps's historic run to eight gold medals and meant that there were many new swimmers looking to join the team in the fall. TSM continued to grow, and we continued to qualify athletes for the most competitive meets in the country. That fall I also passed my doctoral qualifying exams, and by the summer my dissertation proposal was accepted by my committee officially certifying me as a doctoral candidate. I was particularly proud to have been able to excel both as a coach and as a student. Watching Nkechi grind out her projects while she also held down a nine-to-five and acted as a nurturing mother was certainly motivating. What was also fulfilling is that she was equally quick to sing my praises about what I was doing as I was to sing hers. Unfortunately by the time we returned to practice in the fall of 2009, it was increasingly clear that the board of directors was already looking in a different direction.

The first indication that my days with TSM were numbered came when key parents really started to try to pin down my plans for what I was going to do after I graduated from UCLA. I always answered that I planned on coaching as long as I could. I later learned that a narrative was being spun that I was going to leave the team to take a professor job. I also learned that the board members chiefly concerned with shoving me off the plank had already had their replacement of choice come in and meet other key parents during our hiatus. The shit officially hit the fan when the board chairman asked me to coffee after a morning practice early in the season. He told me that the success of the team had afforded the opportunity to go out and hire a big-name coach. An "old gray hair" was the term I'll never forget, and they said that the board wanted to take advantage of the attention our success was drawing to get someone while there was interest. For my efforts, I'd likely get a raise; however, I would no longer be in charge of the group I'd been coaching for four years, and I'd lose many of the administrative duties I had been handling since being named interim coach in 2005. I left that meeting feeling like I'd just been sucker punched. I hadn't been told enough to know when the firing squad would be convened. I just knew that it was coming and that I needed to think of how I was going to deal with that.

I didn't say much about the board's plans to get rid of me for a long time because I knew what kind of circus would start once it became public knowledge and I didn't want to be a part of it. I had witnessed other teams struggle with the transition from one coach to the next, and I saw how it really tore down the team and in many instances forced them to take a step backward. I didn't want that for the swimmers. Many of them I had known since they were eight years old, and after six years they were like my own. I'll never forget when I did address my group and I saw the kids break down into tears. I had a sinking feeling because I wanted to be there for them, but there was nothing I could do despite the efforts of many families who supported me. They lobbied as hard as they could to get the board to rethink their decision. Thankfully as the TSM door closed, another door opened, and I was named the head coach of another club team. The experience was an important one because it was one of those tests where you get to see how strong your marriage really is. I came through that time reassured that my wife would support me through whatever I was facing. There were many nights when I would come home and tell her about the drama of the day on the pool deck, and she would be ready to go out with her hair pulled back and her face full of Vaseline, ready to fight someone because it just didn't make sense to her that I could be fired when the team was doing so well. I eventually just stopped giving her updates because all they did was get her blood pressure up and distract her from the projects she needed to focus on. Her attitude toward the whole situation certainly enabled me to walk onto the pool deck every day with the confidence that even though I'd soon be getting canned, I was going to be okay. I had done my job well. I hadn't choked anybody, and she would be there riding shotgun the whole time.

If Nkechi would've taken the position that it was somehow my fault that this was happening and then stressing every day about what we were going to do with the impending loss of income, I can easily see where the pressure and stress would've built to the point where I would've snapped on somebody and said something or done something regrettable. The fact that I walked the plank with integrity and never sunk to the level of name-calling, e-mail wars, and blog beefs helped me land my next job and has continued to be a reason that I have stayed a part of the SoCal swimming community. Nkechi's support is a big reason for that because she kept me grounded, reassured me so my confidence didn't waver, and didn't add to the pressure that I was already feeling to make sure that I could continue to hold up my end of the bargain financially. She didn't always agree with my approach to dealing with the situation and felt as though in some instances I wasn't defending myself as vigorously as I should have. However, she never really worried about how everything would work out because she decided to lay the burden on God and said that he would work through me to figure out what to do next. She notes that it was a period of great spiritual growth for her because it was such a major situation that she had no control over. All she could do was pray. The level of confidence and trust she showed in me is a key reason why we continue to work as a couple.

June 11, 2011: Celebrating a Championship

Even when the skies were gray,

You would rub me on my back and say, "Baby,

it'll be okay."

Now that's real to a brother like me baby.

—Method Man

On May 27, 2011, I defended my dissertation and concluded what had been a five-year journey to completing my doctoral studies. My mother sat in on the proceedings as did Nkechi. Behind my wedding day and Isaiah's birth, I have never smiled so big or been as overwhelmed with emotion as I was when my doctoral committee of Dr. Megan Franke, Dr. Tyrone Howard, Dr. Ernest Morrell, and Dr. James Stigler gave me the news that my defense had been successful. I felt like I was being launched into the next phase of my life. The part where I would be able to dictate what I wanted to do and how I was going to do it because I had accumulated the kinds of credentials that afforded such opportunities. I could go the route of becoming a tenured professor, or I could become a full-time researcher. I could go back onto a K–12 campus as a teacher/administrator or continue to pursue a career in aquatics. The key was that in adding the Dr. prefix to my name, I didn't have to settle for just anything. If I didn't find an institution that I wanted to call home. then I could strike out on my own buoyed by the knowledge and skills I had gained pursuing my degree. Outside of the professional ramifications, finishing my degree also had deep family connections that added to the emotion of the day.

My dad was giving me a lecture one day when I was about twelve years old for something I had done wrong, and he was talking about aspirations and the type of disciplined life I needed to lead in order to be the kind of man he and my mother expected me to become. I'll never forget that he asked me, "What do you want to do when you grow up?" At the time my world revolved around sports, but subconsciously I must've understood that education was the family business, so I answered, "A gym teacher." At the time I thought that was the coolest job ever. You played games all day, and you got to wear sweats and sneakers to work. What could be better? I thought this was going to send John C. Carroll into a whole new tirade, but he was surprisingly cool with it. He broke it down how PE teachers actually have to have knowledge of the body similar to the level of medical doctors and that if that's what I wanted to do, then I had to be committed to it. That lecture actually turned in my favor because whatever I had done wrong was no longer at the front of my dad's mind. The fact that I actually had a halfway decent career path in mind had made him proud.

My mother, on the other hand, was not as happy to hear that teaching physical education was my career aspiration. She envisioned having a doctor in the household. Her brother, my uncle, Reverend Dr. Harold Fletcher Cottman III, had provided a blueprint for making this happen. He had gone to Central High School as I did, and then on to Harvard. He later earned his MD from the University of North Carolina at Chapel Hill and he was one of my idols when I was little. For my mother, the investment that had been made in my education by sending me to GFS meant that a career as a teacher wasn't enough of a return. I understood that. So by the time I graduated Central High School with the 254th class, I had put aside the notion of being a gym teacher and looked to become an orthopedic surgeon. When I had to take organic chemistry as a junior at Penn, I was faced with the cold reality that many premeds encounter when they enter this notorious "weed out" course. If you don't love science enough to focus and make it through organic chemistry, then being a doctor is probably not the career path for you. The course required the type of passion and discipline that as soon as you left the lecture, you needed to go and play with the molecule kit that is required for the course. Then you needed to go to every small group session so you could understand how to work through the problems of how the molecules rotate and connect. *Then* you could go home and do your homework so that you could be ready for the *next* lecture. It wasn't for me. And when my mother realized I wasn't going be an MD like Uncle Harold, I know there was a small part of her that was disappointed. To have her there at my dissertation defense to *see* how I had gained doctoral-level skills and understanding in the field of education, the very field she had just retired from, had to be a viable consolation prize.

As a father, finishing my PhD models a couple things I want Isaiah to understand as he grows up. The first is that education is everything. It is the most valuable tool available to obtain the social capital necessary to survive in this world, and I want him to understand that the more knowledge you can acquire, the more opportunity you have to dictate what you want to do. He doesn't have to go the formal route that I went, but he needs to always be a seeker of information. The second thing is that there is a Carroll family legacy of excellence in education that he will be expected to uphold. Both my parents hold master's degrees plus additional credits. Nkechi holds a master's degree in economics. In the same way I benefited from my parents' experience and obtained a doctorate, he will be expected to use the cultural cache that Nkechi and I have accumulated between us as a springboard to take the family legacy even further. One of the most memorable pictures I have from graduation day is of four-year-old Isaiah wearing my doctoral tam and hood and grinning from ear to ear. It showed me that he understood that there was an importance to the regalia and that he wanted to share in it. It was one of a handful of memories from that day that helped launch Nkechi and I into the foundation phase of our marriage.

I graduated from UCLA on June 11, 2011, and was ceremonially hooded by my two key advisors, Dr. Megan Franke and Dr. Tyrone Howard. Even though I had already defended my dissertation and gone through the process of archiving it at the library, the UCLA chapter of my life didn't feel complete until the moment they draped that sash over my robe. It's similar to when you watch the Olympics. Winning an actual event brings out sheer exuberance of realizing a goal, but getting that gold medal on the stand and seeing your flag raised as the national anthem plays makes the experience complete. It was fitting that Dr. Franke and Dr. Howard got to present me with my medal because without the two of them, the UCLA experience may not have ever happened. I had applied to UCLA in 2004 when we first moved to California and was not accepted. Once I started teaching at Seven Arrows and coaching, the thought really never crossed my mind. Then I met Megan Franke, who at the time was the head of Center X at UCLA. The Center housed the teacher education program. In addition, she was a faculty member in the urban schooling division of the graduate school. Her daughter, Tessa, swam on TSM. The funny thing about our connection is that it took us running into each other at a lecture Seven Arrows hosted to start talking education instead of on the pool deck. We started talking, and after I told her about being rejected from UCLA, she told me I needed to apply again. She felt that my interests fit better with the urban schooling division as opposed to the division to which I had applied previously. We set up a meeting to talk further, and she introduced me to Dr. Howard, who had done research in many of the areas that I was interested in, particularly the experience of Black males in schools.

That meeting started a five-year ride the three of us would take during which they shepherded me along the path to obtaining my degree. They had the unique understanding of where my life was and what my obligations to my family were. Megan understood my swim team duties and helped me plan how to get things done around the swim calendar. Tyrone understood what it was like to be a student and a father, as two of his four kids were born while he was completing his graduate studies. With all the time and care they had put into my progress over five years, graduation day was not complete without their imprint. In a PhD program, you are basically a glorified research apprentice. Your objective is to learn the craft of conducting research in a certain field and subarea of that field. It is unlikely that you will be accepted into any PhD program regardless of the field unless you have someone who is willing to vouch for you when admissions decisions get made. If you have two people on your side, all the better for you. I will always be indebted to them for being on my team and teaching me so much about the profession beyond the classroom. Both of them, through their actions and conversations that we shared, gave me a good look behind the curtain of the academic machine so that I could make an informed choice about how I wanted to proceed when I was done. When I walked off the stage after I hugged them both and shook the hand of the Graduate School of Education and Information Sciences dean, I was confident that I had been prepared to stand on my own as an educational researcher. When the ceremony ended, I was all set to celebrate reaching the pinnacle of my field just like any team that has just won a championship.

It should be no surprise that Nkechi is skilled at planning an event. Surprise parties are her thing, as she gets a certain amount of extra glee from not only putting together a room and securing food and drink but also getting that look of surprise from the guest of honor when they realize that the little event they thought they were going to is something much bigger. For my graduation it was enough for me that my immediate family was all in town. My understanding was that we were going to go to a nice dinner and that then I would maybe catch up with some of my graduating classmates later. Nkechi had something different in mind, and when I walked into the restaurant with Isaiah and my father, I was shocked to see eight tables filled with friends there to celebrate my graduation. Mike flew out from Philly to be there. My brother-in-law, Okey, came out from New York with his girlfriend. It was overwhelming because they were all people who had constantly given me words of encouragement over the years and had supported Nkechi and me in some way as we tried to make it all work. Lauren Thibodeaux was there, representing for her family who had adopted us for holiday dinners when we didn't go east. David Solomon and Carla Kettner, who were swim team parents at TSM, let Nkechi and me house-sit for them when the TV show David was directing took the family to Canada for six months. They also let Nkechi use the house as the main location for her short film *Bathroom Break*. When I finished scanning the room and taking in the crowd, I looked at Nkechi and said, "You got me." She would've needed surgery to smile any wider than she was at that moment. Little did she know that there was also a surprise in store for her.

By the time June 11 rolled around, Nkechi had fully immersed herself in the world of television writing. When she finished the *Soar* script in 2009, she began to write scripts for television. Some were scripts for shows already on the air to show that she could write in the voice of the show and in the genre. These spec scripts helped her gain attention from potential agents, and she also used them to apply to writer's programs offered by the major networks to bring fresh writing voices into the profession. Nkechi also wrote original scripts to demonstrate that she had fresh ideas for shows that should be on the air. The script that she prized the most and ultimately was her golden ticket into the writing world was called *The Fed*. It was based on her experiences working in the

Federal Reserve system and can best be described as a cross between *The West Wing* and *Grey's Anatomy*. When she finished it and started to get it in front of her industry friends, the feedback was positive. On the recommendation of one of her friends, she sent the script to a mutual acquaintance, Adesuwa McCalla, a manager of writers who was just striking out on her own. She was just supposed to be giving the script a cursory glance, but she liked the script so much that she asked Nkechi if she could represent her. Nkechi had previously met with another agent who liked the script but wasn't going to be able to give Nkechi the level of attention that she would need. Nkechi also liked the plan that Adesuwa laid out to get her on the staff of a show, so she signed with her for a year to see how it played out.

The script for *The Fed* wasn't finished in time to get into circulation so that Nkechi could potentially be staffed on a show for 2010, but Adesuwa got right to work setting up meetings so that Nkechi could get face time with key decision makers who could influence the people who end up in the writer's room for a given show. It was during this season of meetings that Nkechi recognized that she had found her place in the industry as a writer.

She met with executives from *Grey's Anatomy*, and at some point during the meeting it dawned on her that she had been working since we had been in LA to get a meeting like this and that it had never materialized. Within a year of writing *The Fed*, here she was listening to executives from the show gush about the uniqueness of her voice and how much they liked the script. These executive meetings gave her hope that when the 2011 hiring season came around (April to June), she might find a spot on a show. She also knew that it took more than executives being fond of you as a person to secure a job.

Television shows are run by people called show runners who are generally the creators of the show and control most of what happens therein. Shonda Rimes, for example, runs *Grey's Anatomy*. She oversees staffing. She deals with the studio and the network overseeing the show. There are also executive producers that report to her for various areas of the show. So in the same way it's key for actors to get in front of casting agents, it's important for writers to get in front of show runners and executive producers because those are the people you end up working with. Getting in the door to see these people becomes more complicated when you're talking about a show because agents get involved to make the process less accessible. Most shows that make it to television have a show runner who is represented by one of three major agencies in Los Angeles. In order to keep getting work for their clients, an agent will try to get as many writers as they can onto the show. So if Shonda Rimes is represented by CAA, they will try to get as many CAA writers on the staff as they possibly can. This practice makes it very difficult for the writer who has no major representation to get in the door. Both Adesuwa and Nkechi knew this was the mountain they had to climb, which is why Adesuwa set up as many meetings as she could so that Nkechi could have as many chances as possible to get on a show. I started calling Adesuwa Rick Ross after a while because *every day she was hustlin'* for Nkechi. There was even one story where Adesuwa allegedly saw an executive in a clothing store and chased her down before she entered the dressing room in order to pitch Nkechi to her. The hard work paid off because Nkechi eventually had a great meeting with Hart Hanson, the creator and show runner for *Bones*, the longest running show on the Fox

Network. Nkechi had read and liked the script for his new show, *The Finder*. Nonetheless, she was happy to finally get an audience with a show runner. When Adesuwa got up at the party and was the first person to offer a toast, I thought it was strange, given the occasion, but I sat back and listened with my champagne glass ready to hoist it high.

Adesuwa nervously started her speech by talking about how she admired my partnership with Nkechi and noted how she used to receive postcards from her grandmother. Her favorite of these cards read, "Behind every good man there is a surprised woman." Throughout the speech the energetic Adesuwa seemed particularly giddy, and as she reached the conclusion and asked everyone to raise their glasses, it became apparent where the extra happiness was coming from. She closed saying, "We celebrate today as Jon, our successful man, receives his doctorate, let us also celebrate his partner, Nkechi, *the newest staff writer on Fox's new show The Finder!*"

I instantly remember saying, "I knew it!"

Nkechi screamed, "Oh my God!" and then the tears started to flow from both of our faces.

Adesuwa put the cherry on top of her speech by saying, "And there is your surprised woman!" In that instant it made sense that Adesuwa had delivered the first toast and explained her uncharacteristic nervous energy. She had gotten the call earlier that day that Hart Hanson wanted Nkechi on his staff and what better time to deliver the news than at my reception where both of us now had reason to celebrate. I was so glad that David and Carla Solomon were there so that they could share in the raw euphoria of the moment. Carla had worked with Hart Hanson for many years on *Bones*, and when Nkechi told her that she had met with him, Carla went and offered her endorsement to Hart. Between the quality of Nkechi's portfolio, the way she presented herself in person when they met, and having people like Carla to vouch for her, she had earned her golden ticket into the entertainment industry. Our lives had changed in that instant like when a college athlete gets drafted into the pros. June 11 has since been like a holiday for me because in 2011 the trajectory of our lives changed drastically and goals that we had set years before had been realized.

Part 3

The Foundation Years

The Foundation Years

And for love's sake, each mistake, ah, you forgave,

and soon both of us learned to trust.

Not run away, it was no time to play.

We build it up and build it up and build it up.

—Ashford and Simpson

Great teams are built upon certain philosophies that become synonymous with the team and their legacy. The *Showtime* Lakers, the *Bad Boy* Pistons, and the *Steel Curtain* Steelers are all teams that come to mind because the way that they played became part of their championship legacy. A successful family has similar hallmarks that become a part of their lasting legacy. As Nkechi and I embarked on a new chapter, it meant that we were finally in a position to start adding to our foundation that was built on love and friendship and craft a legacy that our grandchildren would be able to enjoy.

The key components of that legacy are love, integrity, financial proficiency, and educational excellence.

Love

We're not just talking about the *eros* or romantic love that a couple experiences when they are first falling for each other. We're talking about an *agape* love. Agape love is characterized by self-sacrifice and completeness. It's the "flaws and all" kind of love that helps keep marriages and families together. In observing how my parents and siblings all gather as often as possible for milestone events, Nkechi noted how "not even divorce" could break up the bond of my nuclear family. We want our sons to have that kind of love not just for their family but also for their kin. When we mention kin, we are referring to their cousins, aunties, and uncles, who have been a part of their lives since birth. This type of love keeps you grounded and humble. You're loving not because you expect something in return but because that is who you are. The powerful thing is that agape love is a choice. It is not bestowed upon everybody. When you can love someone with an agape-type intensity, then you are able to also persist through the times when the other types of love ebb and flow.

Educational Excellence

Education is one of the great equalizers in this country. Sadly the opportunities for a quality education are becoming more exclusive as the institution of public education crumbles in on itself. Nkechi and I will do whatever we need to do in order to make sure that our children are afforded the types of educational opportunities that will enable them to build a cache of cultural capital so that they can pursue whatever makes them passionate. Nkechi and I are living proof of what happens when one is afforded a quality education, and we expect our children to climb up our backs and stand on our shoulders to build upon the foundation we have laid down for them. Education for our boys is particularly important because Black boys exist in this country as targets to be detained or even disposed of the minute they display behaviors perceived as threatening, such as carrying iced tea and a bag of Skittles or playing rap music too loudly. In essence, we're not just talking about a classroom education. It is a specific education on life that is critical because it is the difference between my sons becoming doctoral candidates or inmates.

Financial Proficiency

It is one thing to start making money. It is another thing to know what to do with it once you have it. The instinct is often to start amassing status symbols to complement the lifestyle you think that you can now live. It is much sexier to go out and buy a new car than it is to start an IRA. Going on a lavish vacation is way more fun than saving 20 percent of every paycheck. We want to be the couple that can withstand a writer's strike and not have to worry that we won't be able to pay school tuition. We want to have the type of handle on our budget so that we won't have to wonder if we'll be able to go on vacation because we've already planned for the money being available when we need it. We also want to be intelligent enough that we put our money into investments that are not high risk and will likely result in a loss for us. We don't want to have the attitude the Yankees often display where they will overpay to get a certain player and not really care if the player is a bust because they've got plenty of money coming in. We want to do smart things with the money we accumulate so that we maximize this investment. The couples I interviewed added the following:

Ali—I plan to leave my kids 100 million dollars. Fifty apiece, so as far as money is concerned, providing for them financially, that's my goal.

Royale—I think that it's very important for us to make sure that the kids leave the house with a solid education, college educated, foundation, spiritual base, clear understanding about what their responsibility is, not just what their responsibility to society is as a man, but what their possibility is, which is more important to me.

Terrance—We just recently had the conversation around establishing that W brand and that being something that represents strong family. Not even necessarily dynasty, financial business and all that stuff. That's not something either one of us aspire for. What we aspire for is really low key. Pretty much we want to live and maintain this pretty much standard of living we have right now.

Nkechi and I make a great team because we continue to try to improve as partners who will complement each other. We are also constantly checking in so that we have a good idea of what kind of improvements we need to make. For example, as our careers have developed, I have had to become better around the house and with the kids, and she has had to let go of some of that control. I periodically ask if she's doing okay shouldering the bulk of the financial burden because if I need to work more, I am open to it. As with sports, you can't get complacent in marriage when you get to a good place. You win one championship, and then you have to work just as hard, if not harder, to win the next. There will be periods of struggle or losing streaks that make communication critical to get back on the right track. I know what is critical for me when we argue or disagree is to take time to really reflect on what I am upset about, what my role is in the disagreement, and how we can fix things. This approach keeps our losing streaks from becoming lost seasons. It is very easy to fall into the mind-set that you've known the person so long that you know how he or she will react to something and you don't have to do as much work. That is a trick because we are always changing, so what worked today to resolve a situation might not work next week.

The constant change and development that happens in marriage is why I like the idea of renewing vows annually. Each year really is worth celebrating, and coming up with new vows will send you out into the next year with focus. We have been blessed to build a network of friends with whom we can celebrate each milestone, and for them we are thankful. You heard from some of them in this book, and there will be more in the next. Until then, keep your team going and make sure you and your franchise player stay satisfied.